# A **ZOO** NEAR YOU

# A **ZOO** NEAR YOU

poetry by robert johnson

selected & introduced by chris miller

with contributions by

jennifer adger
liz calka
ania dobrzanska
seri irazola
chris miller
eleanor potter
&
sonia tabriz

cover design by liz calka

text design by sonia tabriz

BleakHouse Publishing

2010

**BleakHouse Publishing**
NEC Box 67
New England College
Henniker, New Hampshire 03242
*www.BleakHousePublishing.com*

Copyright © 2010 by Robert Johnson

ISBN-13: 978-0-9797065-6-1
ISBN-10: 0-9797065-6-4

Printed in the United States of America

For my students,

who are a wonderful and seemingly unending
source of inspiration.

# ACKNOWLEDGMENTS

I am deeply grateful to the American University students, past and present, represented in this volume, each of whom is named on the cover and whose biographical sketches are included at the end of the book. Their contributions – cover design, poems, illustrations, and introductory essay – make this book a tribute to them. I am proud of each and every one of them and honored to have my work associated with them. I also thank Shirin Karimi, an American University student and herself a wonderful writer, for proofreading the book with great care.

The contributions of three of my students stand out and deserve special mention. Chris Miller read all of my published poems and selected and introduced the poems in this book. His introductory essay, Forgotten Souls, is a beautifully written and deeply touching tribute to my work, for which I am grateful. Liz Calka produced an original and engaging cover that is a work of art in itself. I thank Calka for her poems as well, which fit nicely in the early portions of the book, helping establish a context for understanding crime and punishment from the point of view of officials and not just offenders, who for better and worse form the core voice of this book. Finally, Sonia Tabriz produced vivid illustrations and lyrical poems on subtle, existential themes, reflecting her remarkable intellectual maturity and originality. Tabriz generously allowed me to reprint one of her award-wining poems, and jumped in at the last minute to help me pull together the closing section of the book. As this book is readied for publication, I feel a special debt to her for bringing this project to a fruitful conclusion.

The poems reprinted in this book come from various sources but primarily the following: *Poetic Justice* (Conservatory of American Letters, 2004), *Burnt Offerings* (BleakHouse Publishing, 2007), *Sunset Sonata* (Brandylane Publishers), *Admit2*, *BleakHouse Review* and *Tacenda Literary Magazine*.

# CONTENTS

## III.  Big House

## IV.  Death House

## V. Carnage and Consequences

## VI. Closing Thoughts

# Forgotten Souls
## *by Chris Miller*

The realm of incarceration is one of the most destructive and yet least understood aspects of American culture. Much of what is known about prisons is derived from sensationalist media portrayals or comfortable stereotypes. This book challenges that foundation and seeks to give a voice to persons who have been exiled from mainstream society. Robert Johnson's incisive poetry provides a harrowing portrait of the prison experience. Imbued with a stark realism and vivid imagery, it places the reader in the midst of a prisoner's reality. What emerges is a world of mindless bureaucracy, overcrowded cages, debilitating solitude, and indifferent and even abusive officials, themselves often overwhelmed or undermined by the system. We learn that, much too often, our criminal justice system is one of concentrated hatred, devoid of light, and determined to dehumanize its occupants.

Despite the best efforts of this oppressive, often brutalizing environment, Johnson forces us to confront the continuing humanity of those enclosed within it. In his poems, the violent world of the prison yard is intertwined with an exploration of the common human longings for love, companionship, and the self-respect that stems from having even the most tangential control over your own life. Johnson proves that even at its worst, incarceration cannot eradicate these essential human emotions. From destructive sexual relationships between inmates, to the erratic eruptions of prison violence, these phenomena are explored from a new and thoughtful perspective that illuminates the inner struggles brimming beneath them. Prisoners are accustomed to living as forgotten souls; disregarded as time continues in their absence. Robert Johnson's seemingly unlimited capacity for empathy defies abstractions, and presents the occupants of the prison world in their genuine, unvarnished form, for the consideration of our hearts and minds.

Yet, the scope of these poems exceeds a revelation of the human tragedy exemplified by our prison system. The portrait of prison life is complemented by an exploration of the causes of incarceration and the societal attitudes that serve to perpetuate our current punitive philosophy. The emotional impact of these poems is aided exponentially by Johnson's remarkable ability to adopt the voices of his subjects. Whether it be a meandering drug addict or self-righteous cop, readers feel a sense of intimacy and truth that comes from the ability to transcend the words of a gifted poet and truly embody the person being described. Without comment or explicit interpretation, these people are allowed to speak for themselves, in their own distinct voices. Once they are heard, one emerges with a deep emotional understanding of their perspective and how it has shaped their eventual role in the prison system.

Still, true understanding of the prison experience can only come with comprehension of the forces that sustain it. To that end, this collection of poems examines the unsettling prevalence of narrow minded schemes of retribution, with their unilateral focus on harsh punishments. In this restrictive view, espoused ironically in many poems, the underlying causes of crime are ignored in favor of the rapid banishment of its purveyors. As the poems give voice to these convictions, they chronicle the development of a system based on mandatory minimum sentences and a multibillion-dollar industry devoted to warehousing human beings. Beyond the walls of prisons, the poems also comment upon the extension of this so-called "prison mentality" into other areas of American life, including education, homeland security, and foreign policy.

The unfolding of this current state of affairs is played out in counterpoint to the proposal of a new, contrasting vision. Robert Johnson proposes a system that acknowledges the intrinsic humanity and potential in all people, including our worst prisoners. Such a system focuses on the use of punishment to maximize the current and future potential of all prisoners. In this world, the commission of a serious crime does not preclude the possibility of making a positive difference in life. Johnson does not ignore the reality of brutal crimes. Yet, his entire book is a testament to the horrific results of fighting crime with dehumanization and repression. He challenges us to look beyond retribution and cultivate the humanity in those whom we seek to condemn. As we consider this challenge, we must confront one central decision that is best encapsulated in his closing poem: "Reconciliation or revenge? On this choice, our future may hinge."

# I.

## PERSPECTIVE

# A Zoo Near You

A decent zoo captures,
in miniature, the
natural environs of the
animals within.

Prisons don't capture
the free world of the
ranging felon.

They turn that world
upside down and
inside out.

If prisons were more like zoos
maybe we'd visit them
and share our families
and our food
with the captives.

# Poetic Justice

Build prisons
Not day-care
Lock 'em up
What do we care?

Hire cops, not counselors
Staff courts, not clinics
Wage warfare
Not welfare

Invest in felons
Ripen 'em like melons
Eat 'em raw, then
Ask for more

More poverty
More crime

More men in prison
More fear in the street

More ex-cons among us
Poetic justice

# the numbers speak
*by Liz Calka*

| | |
|---|---|
| 2.3 million | (people in the United States confined) |
| 1 for every 100 | (adults in our country) |
| 1 in 10 | (children have a parent in prison, on probation, or on parole) |
| 1 of every 100 | (prisoners will be raped; many more will remain silent) |
| 3,400 | (prisoners wait on death row) |
| 2,225 | (juveniles sentenced to life w/o parole; aka, death by incarceration) |
| 73 | (of those children sentenced to death by incarceration at age 13 or 14) |
| Hundreds of billions | (of dollars spent on punishment) |
| The whole thing a 22. | catch |

## Zero Tolerance

Zero tolerance
Zero common sense

I'm a pro
Don't need to know

Context?
Complex!

It's the rule
It's the law
Don't tell me more.

## No Zone
*by Sonia Tabriz*

## Politics

We hate second thoughts
and the thoughtful people
who think them,
As if a mind can't be
changed
without being
short-changed

# Mother's Milk of Amnesia

Mandatory time
Least we can do

Fight crime
Sacrifice a few

Toe the line
You'll be fine

A little slack
In your plan of attack?

Go back
To square one

Like nothing else matters
Since Day One

Mandatory Hell
Least we can do

Give you a cell
Reserved for two

You
And the horse you rode in on

## What goes around, Or,
## A sewer runs through it

gray, gloomy stone wall
hulking, soaring

silver, shiny metal wire
sharp, gleaming

bare, barred steel cage
barren, bleeding

aluminum commode
cold comfort

flush
whoosh
discharge

They all
get out
They all
come back

Bringing
a little bit of prison
with them

# II.

## CRIME AND PUNISHMENT

# A Gun to the Head

A gun to the head,
a religious rite
in the Church of Crime,
Leaves a smudge
the size of a bullet hole.

Robbers in black,
heads hooded
guns drawn,
make collection.

 "Gimme what you got, man.
It's for a good cause –
'cause I said so."

That's what they might say in the movies.
In real life, they sidle up next to your son
on a dark street, no one else around,
Flash the gun, say "Understand?"
Then, "On your knees!"

Supplicant, eager to appease,
head bowed, digs deep
praying for release
moving as if in sleep
by rote, taking note
of crazy facts,
like the cracks
in the sidewalk,
moving, growing,
now wide enough
to swallow him whole,

Delivered, if he is blessed with luck,
this side of heaven's shore,
of worldly goods and nothing more.

 "Is that all you fuckin' got!"
"Yeah, that's it"
"That's it!?
You just searched me, he thinks,

oddly detached, saying nothing,
as they run off into the night
leaving him alive, somehow, alright.

And the universe, blind, stumbles on
As if nothing at all were wrong
Dad out for an evening's walk
Mom visiting down the block
Brother shooting hoops by the light of the porch
Girlfriend (now wife) waiting for the nightly talk...

Everyone that matters
lost in mundane matters
while the planet had just now
spun on its axis, turned its celestial prow
moved one rotation faster
a hair's breath from disaster.

## Police line: Do not cross

Bright yellow bands
bind the black night
corralling chaos
containing confusion
communicating in cold chorus:

Caution, stand back, stay clear
something terrible has happened here.

Lights, sirens, suits
action, but too little,
too late
too bad.

Lines have been crossed
lives have been lost
long before the police
were called to the scene.

It'll take more than tape
to staunch the blood
bind the wounds
make us whole
when we can't
police ourselves.

## Busted

Busted, sittin' in a squad car
knowin' you're gonna go far.

In a manner of speaking,
this wasn't the life you were seeking.

You thought you'd make a big score
Now you face the prison door

held wide open,
just for you
by the men & women in blue.

In a split second
your life was
split in two.
You'll never be one again,
never be just you.

You're the person you knew
and a criminal, too.  Down the road,
even you will confuse the two.

Maybe you're not a big offender
maybe not a bad one, either.
Only time will tell.
But once we tag you a criminal
we hate to let you go.

So this much you do know:
Nothing will ever be the same.
Your world moves in slow mo'
unfolds in a different frame.

Busted, sitting in a squad car
hands cuffed tight, wrists red and lined,
looking in the rearview mirror
at the life you left behind.

# Squad Car
## *by Eleanor Potter*

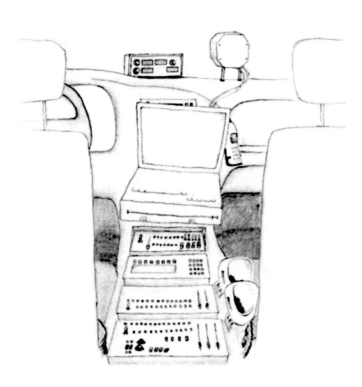

# the law
*by Liz Calka*

I.
When my father came home from work, I would hear his boots
on the dining room floor as he left his 40 caliber Glock to rest on
the top of my mother's china cabinet.
That's where it always was, where young children with big
imaginations couldn't reach it.  Rather than observing
the hole it was burning through the oak,
the danger it presented,
the ticking time bomb it really was,
I used to forget it was there.
Playing with his handcuffs (toys) instead, laughing as he
pretended to arrest me
remembering the time he visited my 3rd grade classroom and
showed us how to dust a plate for fingerprints,
feeling proud.


II.
I never thought twice about the fact that my father
was a police officer
until I became a teenager, trying to
accept the conflicting images that
were being presented to me.
Now I edge around that china cabinet
with caution, avoid walking past it
whenever possible.
I see my father leave in the morning,
ready to save the world,
and now I understand the heaviness of his boots as he
traipses into our dining room after work.
I see the weariness in his eyes.

## Come as you are

Come as you are
Our place ain't far
We'll take you
in our squad car.

Black and white
Lights flashing
Sirens blaring:

We'll wake up the night
Shake up the 'hood
Something's not right
Now we know you're no good.

What did you do?
In your boxers and tee
In your ratty slippers and messy 'do
In that face so flushed and puffy
Maybe tear-stained, too.

Did you beat your wife?
Take a life?
Break and enter?
Assault with a knife?

Truth to tell
You look guilty as hell
Get an attorney,
it'll be a long journey.

# An Addict's Lament

Heroin's his heroine
long, languorous, a loyal followin'

Cocaine's her flame
burns high, hot, never tame

Crack's everyone's whore
like a street walker, an easy score

Addiction's the action
ecstasy the traction
Where the chemical meets the road
helps you carry your load

Live for the high
Enough to get by
Life on the fly

Drug's the main man
no care, no plan
Kill the pain,
do it again

High's your niche,
let's you scratch that itch
Bleeds the strife out of you
Bleeds the life out of you

A shoot up
A shoot out
Death the only route out

# Deadly

Needle, dart
Bull's-eye
Right to the heart

Gun, lead
Deadeye
Right to the head

Sad refrain
Never again

Sole shot
Soul shot

One less
To think about

## Dope

Coke crazy
reefer lazy
life hazy

An existential fog

Sadness sprouts
like wild weeds,
so much burning brush,
hope gone up in
smoke

That's why they call it
dope.

## overdose

living ghost
friends past
lives fleeting
moving fast
head in flight
speed of light

even when you fly
right
you just can't get
right
without another high
right?

living ghost
friends past
lives cast
moving fast
head in flight
speed of light

big vein
speeding train
right to the brain

good buy
goodbye

# Addiction
*by Sonia Tabriz*

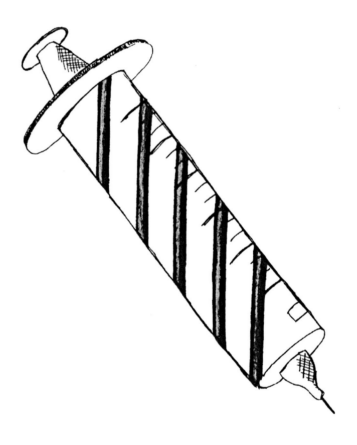

# Gateway
### *by Chris Miller*

They say weed is a gateway drug.
Gateway to peace.
Gateway to happiness
Gateway out of this reality.

Tranquil breezes fill my mind.
Beauty of a blank slate.
Purity of a life without travails.
Nothing crushes my bliss, in the gateway.

Weed tells me I am good.
Only weed can vanquish poverty, extinguish betrayal.
Leave the existential me
Suspended in a better world.

I want to reclaim my weed
Indulge the promise of security.
The boss say weed is bad.
They send me here to be alone.

Prison can constrain my soul.
But my demons remain.
Nothing can help me.
Nothing but my gateway drug.

# Freudian Streets

pimps in pressed pampers
whores in dirty drawers,
johns looking for love

in all the wrong places
in orifices and faces
so many false traces
of care, seeds of

repressed desire, passion, fire
smoldering subterranean sublimation
driving this sordid underground nation
policed by cops with super egos and twisted notions
backed by rouge-red clubs and dark-black subterfuge
denial, unconsciousness the only refuge

# Young thugs

Gun-toting toddlers
Fresh from mean cribs
Got dibs on survival.

Take your candy
In a New York minute.

## Ageless

If he can pull the
Trigger
He must be a
Bigger, Bolder, Older
Badass
than he looks.

# Nuns with Guns

Nuns with guns
under their Habits,
The next NRA gambit?

Already, we've got
God-Fearing, Man-Fearing
All-American Women
trained to shoot from the heel,
even the stiletto heel
(for dressy occasions).

Why not let nun's draw a bead?
Shoot to heal?
Wound to mend?
Kill to save?

Sister of the Gun
The Ultimate Nun
An Ultimatum of One.

Say your prayers and
pass the ammunition
Save souls
shooting holes
in the body of crime.

Christ Jesus Amen,
Will it ever end?

# Cold

There's King Kong,
big and ugly
&
King Con,
big and bad

Then there's me
I'm the one
Son of Kong
Son of Con
Son of a Gun

Number One

Big, ugly, bad
maybe a little
mad

I come first
second
third

You don't count
take my word

A cold way to
live
Only way I know to
live

'Cause I don't give
a damn
or
an inch

# Colder

An orphaned, motherless child can grow up to be one cold son of a bitch, doomed from birth, disconnected, infected with a cancerous rage that eats him up, then spits us out, hurt and bleeding, maybe dead. There's no 'over the rainbow' for this guy, just one long storm. He lives for revenge – cold world, cold comfort. Every now and again he feels a spark of empathy, like a robot, his circuits misfire, he moves jerkily, almost pausing, then forges ahead. "This is a person, this is wrong. But I'm here now, let's just get it done..."

One cold customer laid his victim out with a blast from a shotgun, the man's own shotgun, as it happens. "Watch out," the soon-to-be-dead man said, "it's loaded." Watch out. Watch me die. He crumpled to the floor, dropped like a puppet on a string, cut down with one swipe. The puppet-man looked up, and with eyes wide said, "Why have you done this to me?" That's what the killer saw in his victim's eyes. "Why have you done this to me?" Robot-man paused, circuits shorting, but only for an instant. "This didn't deter me from the task at hand. I shot him in the chest, finishing him off."

Note: Quotations drawn from a convicted murderer, since executed.

## Coldest

I can take or leave executions. It's not a job I like or dislike. It's a job I've been asked to do. I try to go about every job in the most professional manner I can. If they would stop the death penalty, it wouldn't bother me. If we had ten executions tomorrow, it wouldn't bother me. I would condition my mind to get me through it.

Note: Words of an Execution Team Officer.

# Tithing
"Take the Money and Run"

Witness Enron's end run
to infamy
in which fat cats
played investors
like a symphony,
and employees
like a cheap video game.

Bush-league stuff,
even if Bush
and crew
are clean.

# Fat Cat
*by Eleanor Potter*

# A Patriarch's Protocol

Our Father,
who art in
Headquarters,
Hollow be
Thy Claim.

Thy Fortune Come
Thy Will be Mum
On CNN
and before
Congress.

Lead us Not
Into our Prison Nation,
And Deliver us
From Civil Obligation
to our Fellow Man.

Amen.

# The problem with criminals

We hate criminals
for the harm they do
We love victims
for the hurt they go through

We love criminals
for their rebel ways
We hate victims
for their fearful gaze

Lines here are rarely clear
bruised and blurred by hate and fear
Yet every day made neat and plain
by Lady Justice, in
blindfold and train

# In the Beginning

We were cannibals once,
and hungry,
feeding freely
on the flesh
of our enemies.

War was a long buffet line,
at least some of the time,
in early times,
perhaps more times
than we care to admit or remember.

Sidling up to the salad bar of vanquished foes
we'd pick and choose from the
carnal bounty of killing fields.

Portions of War – Big servings, many choices,
A loin here, a second joint there,
A little brain on the side, always a delicacy.

More victories, more bodies,
more selections, more consumption.
Winners grow fat on the fat of losers,
sucked lovingly from warm, sliced bones.

Eat fast, eat fat, get fat, live large.
It's an old story, maybe the oldest.
To the victor belong the spoils,
eaten soon after they fall, before they spoil.

No treats to be had from sinew
or tendon or bone, but
Victory is always sweet,
a dessert in itself.

And then there are the women.
Kill and eat the men and children,
especially the fleshy ones;
take the women to go.

A grisly, glorious, gory,
unrestrainedly hedonistic business,
this sating of animal appetites,

Which serves as model and metaphor
for capitalism in the raw,
where the rich
kill and eat the poor,

Sucking wealth from their labor
picking their tired bones clean

Living off the fat
of the toiling unclean

Until all that's left
for the hopeless bereft
are illness and early death.

# Hungry for Justice

Suspects are caught, contained,
questioned, interrogated,
derogated;
simmered 'til sufficiently
tender,
ready to serve
time
or have their goose
cooked
moved from frying pan to
fire
seared in the hot
seat
or chilled on a cold
gurney

## Word Play

Deer
Game
Kill
Sport

Dear
Game
Kill
Spat

Assault Rifle
Sport
Hand Gun
Spat

Euphemism
Cynicism
Recidivism

Domestic Violence
Word

# The Angry Marshal
*by Seri Irazola*

On the second day of my internship, the defendants were shuffled out of the lockup cell and into a more crammed and uncomfortable cell behind the courtroom. I was sent to get one final interview. With few exceptions, access to this cell area is restricted to marshals and defendants. As an intern, I was not expected behind those doors. Standing back, clenching my clipboard, I watched in horror as an angry marshal started his daily speech to the defendants:

> "Listen up you motherfucking cocksuckers! You stupid pieces of dog shit! Hey! You nigger over there on the shitter...you best be paying attention to me too! Okay assholes, you are going to stand here as quiet as can be, and when I call your lockup numbers, you are going to walk forward. You are going to follow me into court, and you are going to stand there and lick that judge's ass as if she was your girl! If any of you decide that you are going to play tough, I will bring you back here and not only will I kick the living shit out of you, but I will put you into a cell without windows—where no one can hear you cry, and I promise you that an angry bunch of Marshals will come in there and make you wish you were never born! If you are going to go to jail tonight, and you know this, then take it like a man! We need to get through this quick! No one in here wants you to be fucking it up, because all you motherfuckers have to be seen today! My old lady has dinner on the table at 5:00pm every fucking night. If any of you act up, and I have to stay here to deal with you, my lady is gonna kick my ass, and that means that I am going to have to stay here extra long to pull my boot out of your ass for pissing off my lady! Now, not a fucking word out of you fuckers! Number 4, 78, and 89, step up now!

## Presumption Gumption

We find no atheists on the battlefield
Where death looms
Nor innocents in the court room
Where convictions bloom.

Guilt, that's the presumption
Though we lack the gumption
To admit it straight out.

By the time you get to Court,
No one thinks you're innocent.
No one.  Not really, anyway.
Even your mother has her doubts.

You're dirty, manhandled from day one,
Greasy prints and donut crumbs all over you.
Pushed around, head bent
Kept at arm's length
Cruisin' for a bruisin'
Down for the count.

Cops sniff you out,
paw you around
leave you dazed and numb,
ready for the DA*
the big cat these days,
who direct your sorry ass
to court that fateful day
your corpus (read carcass)
dragged and gagged
(sometimes literally)
before a judge
on high
a robed figure with a big gavel,
an ancient artifact,
polished but pointless,
since His Honor is flanked

by officers with modern guns
and presides over a silent line
of humbled humanity,

fresh from cramped cages,
Unkempt, unrested, uneasy
even queasy,
compliant to a fault.

They've been prepped
Marshals know where they live.

The judge calls all the shots.
Bang, Bang
Order in the Court!
By Order of the Most Honorable Court!
Everyone else goes through the motions,
when you get right down to it,
following his script.

"All Rise," shouts the Bailiff,
Often old and thin,
He might as well say,
"Let the Battle Begin"
and under his breath,
"We're eager to fight
'cause we almost always win."

You, hunched down,
Under a cloud of suspicion,
On the defensive, not called
defendant for nothing,
Relying for your freedom
maybe your life
On a Defense Attorney,
A Public Defender, most often,
Guardian of the poor public,
Green folk who fend off, as best they can,
the formidable forces of justice,
secure in the deep pockets of Uncle Sam.

This is a trial alright, a crucible, a test,
featuring, if you raise your hand
and take the stand,
a cross examination – you,
At the left hand of the father
clearly on the outs,
Hammered by the prosecutor

questioned coldly, crossly
Handled crossly, coldly
fixed in place
for all to see.

Your life an open book,
suspended, spread-eagled
exposed.,

People figure, "God knows,
We'd never crucify an innocent man."

It started at the beginning,
when you talked to the detective.
"Just tell your story," his gentle directive,
like he wants to hear a bedtime tale
after a long day putting people in jail.
But he didn't say, "It will be lights out for you,"
when he offered soft drinks, coffee, gum to chew.
Snack-and-chat hour though
he served the DA none other than you.

Hungrily, she ground your words,
Now called a confession, into nugget-sized
lumps of culpability, easily digested,
fast food for judge and jury,
Who select a sentence
From a list of approved options:

Read carefully, as
The menu has changed.

Settling on an American Standard:
Shake, bake, and serve time.
Easy as apple pie.

Court is a world of words.
Words rule, talk counts.
"I withdraw the question,"
an attorney might say.
Puff, it's gone.
"Ignore that comment."
Voila. Never happened!
"The jury is to disregard..."

the judge intones,
in basso falsetto.
Disregard what?
A bell that rang?
The latest harangue?
The whole panoply of power
paraded before them?

It's like magic,
Black Magic,
Engrossing,
even entertaining,
in a dark way.
A juridical Disney Land,
a modern wonder,
Unless you're the one
Nailed on cross,
Desperately seeking
Redemption.

* DA stands for District Attorney or Prosecutor.

## Her Honor

Each day at nine a.m. sharp,
Justice calls and she answers,
Slipping into her chambers,
Slipping out of her print dress
Into her black robes,
Trading high heels
For sensible pumps.
Her judicial attire:
Sober, authoritative,
Her I'm-always-right getup.
Of this she never tires,
Though some days the robes hang heavy,
Cloth wearing thin in spots.

Pomp and Circumstance, she knows,
Redolent of Raw Power,
Purvey a Palpable
Presumption of Prescience.

Judge not, warns the Bible,
But she does, and is not
Judged in turn:

Much like Royalty
Who held Court
In Times Past,

Much like Superman
Court of Last Resort
Another Caped Crusader.

To err is human, she knows
To forgive, divine.
She makes mistakes,
maybe noted on appeal,
never noted in court, but
She never forgives,
Never forgets.

You're guilty
Or not guilty
Never innocent.

Enter her world, you're tainted
Never again clean.

She lives with that
You live with that
We all live with that.

Uneasily, one can only hope.

# Lady Liberty
*by Jennifer Adger*

# A Bend in the Road to Justice

A quiet moment,
A break in the adversarial engagement;
A young female attorney chats
Amiably with her client, a
Hulking man convicted of capital murder.
Beside them, nominally on duty,
A mustachioed guard, looking like a
Genial refugee from the 1890s,
Smiles, nods, adds a light comment.

Back a few rows and to their right, a
Lone woman, older, sustained
By a long thin oxygen tube, sits quietly,
Deep in mourning for the victims,
Both blood to her, both ripped from her life,
Both missed in a visible, visceral way.
She will be joined by family when court resumes,
And laughter will make quiet ripples in their grief,
Small escapes from the horror that has enveloped them.

They want justice and they may get it
But they'll get no relief, no reprieve,
From their life sentences, shadowed by death,
Lived one long day at a time.

## Sentence Gridlock

He tried to scale the wall, scrambling for a toe-hold
in the formidable edifice of federal sentencing rules,
Rock solid, brought to an angry public
by an over-wrought Congress.

He'd been warned,
it's treacherous stuff, a long fall.

People pay for hard justice
in our Donation Nation.
Go soft, soft money's
hard to come by.

Digging in,
getting a good grip,
He began to chip
away, case by case,
relying on pertinent facts,
sharply on point,

Knocking time off here
tacking on a program there,
Depending
on things like
The person, The crime, The particulars.

Controversial
these days,
Days of the
Justice Infomercial:

Get the latest and greatest sentencing kit,
One sentence fits all, Satisfaction guaranteed
But wait, there's more...

Got his hands slapped, told
Justice is a board game,

like chutes and ladders.
Where you fall
tells it all.

Do the crime,
get the time.
No gray,
least not today.

Tomorrow?
who can say?
Supreme Irony
ever at play.

# Reasonable Doubt

"Guilty beyond a reasonable doubt,"
we intone, a bit smugly, doubting
we know what's reasonable
about reasonable doubt.

Beyond a shadow of a doubt?
Dubious, I'd say, that the sun
shines that directly each day
on us, mere mortals at play
in the game of justice.

Beyond a nagging doubt, like a
stain that won't wash out or go away?
Possible, you say, but too easy
to make the culprit go away,
and with him our doubts allay.

What doubt is unreasonable
for reasonable women and men
judging those who offend?

What reasonable person
has no doubts
in human affairs?

We can arrest and detain
judge and inflict pain
again and again
and be legally right
but dead wrong,
without a doubt.

# Justice Shoppers

Some prosecutors are eager justice shoppers,
Charging everything in sight
Up and down the aisles
Copping one special or another
Scoring one bargain then another
Living for the deals and discounts
Rung up every working day
Ca-ching, Ca-ching.

It's an addiction,
each sentence
pure satisfaction

The cart may be overflowing,
Filled with bargains we can't afford.
But tell that to the DA.
Tab don't go his way
Today or any day.
Only we pay.

## I Witness

An eye witness
is really an I witness.

Who we are, how we feel,
shapes what we see.
Who we become
shapes what we saw.

This see-saw is a
balancing act beyond
any scale of justice.

Yet when we say,
"He's the one"
Our pointed finger's
As deadly as a gun.

# Lineup
### *by Eleanor Potter*

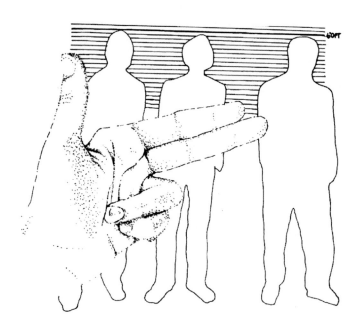

## Super Juror

Up in the court house –
Is it a bird, is it a plane!
No, it's Super Juror!

Foe of prosecutors everywhere,
faster off the topic than a
speeding train of thought,
able to distort tall arguments
with a single leap of faith,
Super Juror metes out justice
on his own terms.

Like Clark Kent, these closet heroes
dress like you or me, but when the chips are down,
they fly off to handle the world's problems,
convicting and exonerating
as the shifting winds move them,
imaginary capes and all,
on rising thermals
and sinking depressions,
eager, but unsteady,
a fickle force
in the fight
for justice.

Note: The term "super juror" is used regularly and derisively by some prosecutors.

# Criminal Justice

To be a criminal is inimical
to your health and well being,
or to your being at all.

Crime pays, sure, but
the hours are long,
good help is hard to find,
and the work can kill you.

Plus we capture most criminals,
then cage them,
first in holes, now in cells.

Some prisoners we flat-out shoot –
in the old days, with any weapon that came to hand,
nowadays with lethal drugs.
Ain't progress grand?

We've come a long way, I suppose,
but a cell's not a home and
dead is dead.

It's criminal, what we do to criminals,
and what criminals do to us.
That's where we get the criminal
in criminal justice.

So where's the justice?

## Loss

Like so many before me,
I take the stand
solemnly, to swear
on my broken life,
my face ashen,
bloated by grief,
my legs moving slowly,
awkwardly,
my head in a fog,
the pain palpable
even now, more than
a year later.

My son is dead,
I am dead.
Life goes on
without us.

His killer sits
before me, in
shackles and khakis,
very much alive.
He may one day walk free.

Not me, imprisoned for life,
My world shrunk to a
grave and a bedroom:
one tended,
one untouched,
both washed
by a river of tears.

My life hangs by a
thread, sewn in sedatives;
numb, desolate
beyond redemption.

Why go on
without my son
my light,

the one
I rose for
each day?

Make his killer's
punishment
a monument
to my loss.

Leave his father a
grave and a bedroom:
one tended,
one untouched,
both washed
by a river of tears.
His life hanging by
a chemical thread;
numb, desolate
as good as dead.

Justice.
Not just us.
Anyone.
Everyone.

An eye for an eye
A blind animal cry
Raw revenge.

## Name Game

They bought your drugs
You sold your life
They made you an offer
you couldn't refuse.
Now you're facing

Five to ten
Ten to life
Life with an out
Life without
Death on a gurney
the ultimate clout.

The ball's in your court
to your own self be true
Rat someone out
get less time to do.
Guilty or not, most
any name will do

Five to ten
Ten to life
Life with an out
Life without
Death on a gurney
the ultimate clout.

They all play the same game
the criminal name game
cops and thugs in the same frame

That's how we fill our prisons
one rat at a time, on
each side of line.

# Adversary Justice

Adversary, enemy
Righteous authority
Subhuman entity
Formula for entropy

Justice grinds slowly
to a dead halt
Vengeance takes flight
on bloodied wings

# Life Sentences

The judge gave him life, we say,
with no sense of the irony

or the arrogance
or the enormity

of sentences given out every day
in court rooms across the nation.

God gave him life.
His mother gave him life.

The judge takes life, condemning
people to cells or coffins,
which are pretty much the same
thing, when you think about it.

# Testilying

White lies
Convicting
Bad Guys

Sending
Sacrifice Flies

To the Prison Wall.

Note:  Seasoned defense attorneys often refer to police testimony in criminal cases as testilying, or routine lying in the course of testimony.

# Custom Framing

Convictions
made to order
Lineups
but no lines
Evidence
cut to specifications
Background
shaded to taste
Exotic
samples, models
Cuffed
buffed, ready to
Mount

Get orders in early
Beat the weekend rush

Repeat customer discounts available
Some jobs require extra time

A service of police predilections,
"Where the truth lies" and
"We stand on our convictions"

# Face it

Faces
Faces Framed
Faces Framed by steel cell bars
Faces Framed by stone and mortar walls
Faces Framed by leather-strapped gurneys
Faces Framed by plain box caskets
Faces Framed
Faces

Faces
Faces Framed
Faces Framed and Mounted
Faces of the Dead
Faces of Justice
Faces Framed
Faces

## Money Talks

Law
Tired old whore
Looking
For an easy score

Legal tender
Hard currency
Money talks
Nobody walks
Without it

Green
Goes free
Black & Brown
Stay down

White
Be right
Keep the bucks
In sight

No bread?
Good as dead

Law
A hard bitch
A cold lay
When you can't
Pay

Note: An old joke about the death penalty goes like this: Only those
without capital get capital punishment.

# Demons One and All

At the bar of justice
Innocence is no bar to
Conviction
Confinement
Condemnation
Consignment
to the junkyard of lost souls.

After the fall
we brand criminals  demons
one and all
once and for all.

Innocent?  Too late,
Too good to be true
A technicality, not fate.
Not the real you.

We swallow our mistakes,
keep them safe and warm
in the belly of the beast
where they belong.

# III.

## BIG HOUSE

# American Dream House

Ah, the American Big House,
Country Club Confinement, Catering
to the Cloistered Criminal Class,
Perennial thorn in the side of those
who bitterly begrudge the lowly felon
his meager lot, really no more than
three hots and a cot.

Oh, thinks the angry person on the street,
to retire at government expense, to be
bound by golden handcuffs and
escorted to gilded cages, to have
meals served daily by a
trained, uniformed staff!

Give me prison any day,
such folk are wont to say.
Lifers have the life!
No work, no wife
no bills to pay!

Next thing you know, our
pouting purveyors of punishment
will pose for pictures, proudly,
with the Loch Ness Monster.

Like that mythical beast,
palatial prisons and
carefree convicts are
creatures not found
in any nation
other than our
imagination.

# Hot House

Prison is the endless summer
of a convict's discontent,
shadeless, hot, unforgiving.

This Big House
This Hot House is
Their House, for
Better and Worse.

Criminals boil with
passion, escaping like
steam, but only from
frying pan to fire.

They come ready for the heat
grilled by cops to a turn,
some with a third degree burn.

A few feral flowers bloom
in our Big Hot Houses,
out of sheer conviction.

Most wilt, hanging limp,
like so many dangling
sentences.

# Prison

Prison
life poisoning
punishment
for people of poverty.

Prison
lash of rebuke
wielded like a whip
on the working wounded.

Prison
dark black
dungeon of despair
denizen of the dispossessed.

Prison
waste dump
for wasted lives,
house of refuge
for human refuse,
warehouse for
worn out,
used up
cast off
careworn creatures,
now humbled and discarded.

Prison
time out
of sight,
time out
of mind,
for those
who don't
toe the line.

# Solitary Soliloquy
## by Ania Dobrzanska

I hear music no one else hears. I see things no one else sees. In a cell alone, I have a whole world before me. In the hole, I am swallowed whole, tortured and tormented, torn apart.

Fear washes over me, cold and close, numbing my limbs, paralyzing my thoughts. Each second a snapshot, exposed, explored, stretched... I feel. I feel a drop of sweat trickle down my pale face. Blood rushes through my veins, pounding in my chest, ringing in my ears; my muscles tense, then cramp. Parched throat like a sandy dessert, thirsty, hungry, exhausted. I've exhausted all senses, now I'm numb. It is me against the world and I am not ready.

I sense them outside my door, lurking. The creaking of steel doors, slow and low, tells me I am at the gates of hell, two devils in military gear my unlikely escort. Like an enormous wave on a raging sea, freezing cold crashes against me, drowning my heartbeat, blurring my vision, stealing my breath.... raping me, leaving me empty, shivering, unmoving, jammed between two worlds, the living... and the dead. Trapped, wedged between terror and rage, I want to fight but I see it, the darkness of the hole, the pit, waiting for me, drawing me down, sucking the life out of me in an instant. I relent.

The hole lives, that I know. I'm scared... I scream, but no one hears. I cry, but no one sees. I hear nothing. I see nothing. I am here but I am gone. I am inside myself, and inside the hole. I am the hole, and the hole is me.

Will I ever be free?

# Pod People

Human husks wrapped in scorn
solitary figures, mute, forlorn
lay flat, unmoving, unmourned
arms crossed, faces slack
eyes half open, glazed, black
tortured on a modern rack.

Buzzers beep, hum, a morning rite
inert figures come to life
a marionette review,
run in mime, lost in time.

Over go pairs of feet,
thwack, thwack,
flat on the floor
Slowly rises each torso,
twisting, creaking,
turning gingerly toward the door
Carefully moves each form,
dragging, shuffling,
inching toward the murky light
Sepia-toned, heavy,
etched in grime, thick with blight
detritus of a long dark night.

Each man, each day, in his way
goes the distance, makes his bones
traversing his cloistered world alone
touring his cell, his private hell
dancing with his demons
dreaming he's a free man.

All this, yet no one knows
no one heeds these one-man shows
one puppet per stage, one prisoner per pod
one guard, on guard
unseeing, unseen

runs the supermax machine;
a padded vest, hands gloved in gray

pushes buttons, shoves trays
recedes, a phantom, into the haze.

People of the Pod,
pomanders and epithets
pressed to sweaty chests like amulets,
breathe deeply of the fetid air,
speak daily to God, Care
only that He use the Rod

"Punish me," they say, "for I am bad."
His Word redounds,
comes off the wall, off the page,
floats in space, feeds their rage,
each cell a terminal stage,
a killing cage, for men

stoned, dazed, left to fate
blinded by a bright white hate,
wallowing in delusion
stewing in corruption
yearning for direction,
to be Somebody
not just some body.

# One Uniformed Woman

In the penitentiary,
she'd tamed lions
without a whip
without a weapon.

She'd whistle,
iron doors rolled
back, out came
the big cats
one per cage
cool, calm, collected
lined up, in a row.

A great show,
Greatest show on earth;
One uniformed woman
starched collar, sensible shoes
in the center ring.

At the supermax,
prison of prisons
she's the tame one,
sliding steamy styrofoam
boxes, filled with chow
into  each cell
through a slot.

Work's hot
collars wrinkle
feet sag
days drag.

"Slide the tray
stay out the way"
that's her day.

Cats stay confined
Lion tamer's resigned
Nothing but hard time.

Nothing super
About supermax
putting guards
in prison.

# Mistress of the Cell Block

She stoops to conquer
slowly removing his jump suit
jumping him in his cell,
No concern for dirt or smell
or who might tell.

A moment free of hell
is what drives him
to her.

She risks it all, but
men on their knees, please
it's hard to resist
She's on a roll
in control.

Gender bends prison bars
with bare female bodies,
launching men into space.
Venus in orbit, Mars rising, a
miracle of modern punishment.

Sex in prison, with men
who've been around the block,
And women who feel free to

Knock on any cell,
any cell at all,
risking it all
For love
in a cold climate.

## Master of the Messhall

He strides imperiously to the serving line,
his serving line, a baton in his ham-sized
hand, tapping it lightly against his leg,
twisting it slightly, with a hint of menace.

"The chow stops here,"
he says with a sneer,
a big man in a
small job, always
a bad situation.

He talks in clipped phrases,
Terse
Tough
Staccato
Bravado.

"Easy on the mash, my man"
he says to a server
who knows the routine
but tests him anyway.

"Hand back that snack, Jack"
he says to a con
who growls
lifts a leg
moves on.

"Easy on the steak, Jake"
another server busted
bold as a brass monkey
adjusting his plastic hair net
shamelessly, like nothing
happened.

"Put down the juice, Bruce"
You've got too much meat to eat
Too much garden in your salad
Too much starch for your march.

He's got it goin' on now, talkin'
Smooth as butter, moving
Slow as molasses
Takin' names and
Kickin' asses.

"This is a prison, mister"
He says to no one in particular.
"If you can't take the heat
Stay offa my beat."

Only he knows
how thin the veneer
how fragile the façade
that gets him through each day.

Petty ain't pretty
but order matters.

Let down your guard
and some cons will
Eat you alive.

# Box Canyon

Those crazy goons, thumping their chests, dancing in jerky motions, shoulders hunched, teeth bared, hootin' and hollerin', making a show of their show of force, telling the caged cons, "we're crazy motherfuckas, maybe as crazy as you, so come out the zoo, do what you got to do." Their prey wants to play, climbs the bars, shakes the cage, burns acrid black with rage, figures "fuck you, I'm tired, I'm bored, I'm pissed, bring it on." Everybody wired, cold stoned on adrenaline, pumped, ready for a little corrective action. Hack and cons, locked in the box,* the hole, the end of the line, ready to get it on, doing time hard before hard time does them, moving to a beat as old as the wild and as new as a fresh wound.

* The box is slang for punitive segregation, a place of great pressure that gives way now and again to ugly confrontations between frustrated officers and inmates.

# A Cell with a View

Shadowy forms mill about aimlessly
oblivious to the stone walls
and razor wire fences
that surround and contain them
like so many cattle at a slaughterhouse.

A whistle blows, ending their fragile freedom.
"The Yard is Clooooosed"
bellows a deep baritone voice.
The words hang in space, then echo
down the concrete canyons of the prison yard.

Herded up and moved out,
led shuffling and murmuring
through cramped corridors
to claustrophobic cages,
their bodies branded by
jagged shards of light from
flickering flourescent tubes
perched menacingly overhead.

Sun light at dusk makes
a forced entry into the cell block,
cutting through motes of dust
like a sharp knife through tender flesh.

Echoes of cell doors closing,
steel on steel, hard, final,
rise to greet the dying light of day,
filtering down rows of cells
stacked neatly like boxes,
but no ribbons or bows,
no prizes or surprises
for the men inside.

A prisoner peers through plexiglass partitions
like an old man with cataracts, his vision
blurred by a waterfall of air holes,
ragged and rough edged,
so many bullet wounds
from a drive-by shooting of the soul.

There by popular demand, each convict
will be held for a long engagement,
sometimes with a few intermissions,
in the theater of wasted lives
we call The Big House, home to the
double-feature creature-classic:
the punishment of crime and
the crime of punishment.

# doing time
*by Sonia Tabriz*

Time
On my mind

Doing my mind
Screwing my mind
Chewing my mind
Into shreds

Bits and pieces
Of a man
That once was
But now is
Nothing more
Than time

Time
On my mind

## Reptile House

Men lie like snakes
coiled tight in bright,
shadeless, barbed-wire run,
shedding shirts
seeking shelter
under searing sun.

Soon, too soon,
called, culled
carried along
colorless corridors to
cloistered cells, cold
cement crevices
dark and dank
close and musky.

Readily, too readily,
slouching, stretching
sliding along
slow, servile
syrupy
like warm spit
oozing lazily into
wide jawed
empty bellied
cages.

Easily, too easily,
flesh tears
souls sunder on
serrated steel bars
industrial strength
teeth, grinding
swallowing, storing
small sacrifices
in the belly of the beast

Late, too late,
animation suspended
pain unended

ROBERT JOHNSON

palpable, pervasive, perpetual, the
perennial price of punishment.

Prison primordial
time immemorial.
The fit may survive
but no one comes out
fully alive.

# Night Owl
### *by Sonia Tabriz*

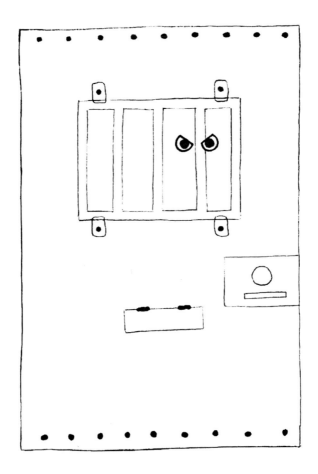

# Signs and Portends from Planet Prison

"All illiterate inmates line up here,"
read the sign on the prison wall.

Another sign warned, "this institution is reserved
for the most dangerous, disruptive and diverse inmates."
Reserved? Diverse inmates?
Has political correctness come to this?

At a women's prison, a sign advertises a long running program:
"Girl Scouts Behind Bars."
As with Prince Albert in a Can,
one can only think, "Please, let them out!"

Female visitors to a supermax prison
are greeted by a sign telling them they may
"only wear skirts of a modest length,"
which in a kind world would mean topless women
in insubstantial, nominal or otherwise skimpy outfits.
After all, hard-core prisoners don't get to see many women.

The other day, after a session in prison,
I stopped for lunch at a Wendy's restaurant.
The sign outside read, "hiring losers."
In bold letters, no less.
Closers might be losers, by some reckonings,
but why rub it in?

The problem, I realized, is bigger than prison,
but perhaps most painful in prison.

"What we have here is a failure to communicate."

That's today's Gospel,
According to Luke,
Cool Hand Luke.

## More from Planet Prison

The inmate refused to "bend and spread 'em'," saying,
"I've never showed my ass to nobody and I ain't starting now."
He was duly reprimanded by Officer Chippendale.

The mail order form in the prisoner's file read:
"Stocking hat, ski mask, ear plugs.  Rush shipment."
The order was processed promptly.

Notation in a prisoner's file, complete and unabridged:
"Parole denied, rehear in 10 years."

Notation in a prisoner's file, under Demographics:
"Dark" "Large" "Christian" "Carpenter"

"Inmate attends church weakly," it was noted in another file.

The fight was serious, we learn in a memo, since the man "went
for the juggler vein." Another fight was ruled "a clear-cut case of
elf defense."

One inmate was punished for "making a para-military jester,"
which may be a comedian in camouflage, a distant relative of the
juggler noted above, or at least someone on good terms with
prison elves.

# Hard Time

I chill out
in cold storage
concrete and steel
my constant companions

My life a
closed cage
suppressed rage
servile submission
sheer survival

On the good days.

Echoes of present and past
things done that can't be undone
bells rung that can't be unrung
swirl in and around me
oceans of regret that
surround me, drown me
'Til I surrender

Every night.

I do time
Time does me
I'm a prisoner
Never free
Ever.

## Rock Pile

On a good day
she dig gems
from the rock pile
of her imagination

Sifting
dirt and dust
for a nugget
of truth

for a diamond
in the rough,
for a glimmer of hope
in the hell she calls
home.

# Light from Another Country

Knife bright light
Fills up the cell, rays
Bouncing off gray cement walls
Piercing his eyes, slicing
Through lids squeezed

Tight against the
Dark night of despair
The hard light of introspection,

Revealing who he is,
Where he is,
What he will become.

In time, a creature of the night,
On the wrong side of right.
He knows this, we know this;
It's as clear as the light
Of day.

## Colossal Corrections Clearance Sale

Starts Today!  3 Great Ways to
Save, Save, Save
On that Prison Cell we've earmarked for you!

This is the Real Deal,
The Big Deal.
The Colossal Corrections Clearance Sale!

Huge selection of models –
Singles, doubles, and more,
Some with a view
All color coordinated
Bars included
On Terms that are a
STEAL.

Plus, our SUPER Rewards Special.
Up to half off on Early Bird selections.
An extra 15% off the top with Bonus Coupons.

Regular Offenders get a 10% Reward Card.

Get-out-of-jail-free cards not accepted with this offer.

# No Vacancies Allowed

You may be innocent
But you won't get one cent
From some jurisdictions
Where predilections
Favor punishment
For its own sake,
Like we have a stake
In the Big House.

No Vacancies Allowed
Say it loud
Say it proud.

## Our Black Prison Nation

At first blush, today's black prisons
look like a green wound, a fresh assault,
something new under the sun.

But Old Hannah* burns hot and relentless
on peoples pushed to the margins,
exposed, defenseless.

This modern conflagration is but a recapitulation
of patterns dating back to our country's creation
seen all too clearly in slave ship and plantation
in share cropper hut and urban underclass station
reaching full flower in our black prison nation.

A world apart, so black, so rife with misery
the prison is utterly foreign to those who be
wealthy, especially white and wealthy,
those paragons of privilege given a healthy
dose of justice in the land of the free.

So it is, as ever, a given:
The rich get richer
and the poor get prison.
Especially in the slums
where color is life's prism.

A lucky few from penal interment
come risen (after three decades, not three days)
but they, unlike Christ,
are unbidden
and unwelcome
in the land where only
           the white,
                   and wealthy,
                           are truly free.

* Old Hannah is a name for the sun in slave and plantation prison songs.

# School House Lockdown

When did we decide that public schools were prisons,
the kinds of places that sported metal detectors, cops,
locks on every door?

Was it when we decided that separate could not be equal?
Or when we decided we were not equal to the task of educating
the whole public, rich and poor, black and white, all together?

Did we abandon our schools when they had to be public schools
rather than private schools run at public expense?

Our prisons are more repressive every day
Our schools are more prison-like everyday

Freedom?
Just another word for nothing left to lose?
Janis?
Janus?
Shame on us.

## No-where Men

A prisoner is a
no-hole mouse          Behind
no-mercy walls         In
no-hope cages.

He's got a
no-future life         In a
no-home world          With
no-where to go         But
hole-up in prison.

# Supersize My Prison, Please

Like to Supersize that prison, mister?

You betcha!  Sounds keen!
Bigger, bleaker dungeons –
More punishment, more green.

Prisons, cheaper by the pack,
Prisoners, a bargain by the million.
Lock em up and don't look back.
Think of prison as an underclass cotillion.

Who said America didn't have balls?

## Failure, Fickle Friend

Nothing succeeds like hard-won failure
Did my best, can't do no better
Leave things be
Just fine with me
It's God's will
(or some such swill)
So chill
It's the bitter pill
We call Life

Failure
Fickle friend
Gives cover
To fail again
And again,

Distracting us
From the Suite life
To the Street life.

Sweet
For the folks on
Easy Street,

Conferring freedom to freely
Lock poor people up and
Lower the boom, 'til
There's just no room
At the Inn,
And we mark the narrow prison cell
The poor man's due reward in hell.

His smoldering resentment
Our smug contentment
The way of the world
The path of least desistance
When Failure is your Fickle Friend, giving

Congenial cover
When you lower
The boom.

# All you convicts

All you convicts gather round
to hear a tale of great renown,
of young boys raped and old men cowed,
In golden days when convicts bowed
to no man
no where
no how

and staff knew their place
and cons knew the score
and weak was just another word for whore
for folk who'd bend over backwards
to get out the door.

# Cell block serenade

Hey, Hey
he's my little Sheila
tattoos and a pony tail.

Love a little fem
like my little Sheila
man that little con is fine
you know I got to make her mine.

Hey, Hey
he's my little Sheila
her mane
drives me insane.

Love a little fem
like my little Sheila
man that little trick is mine
even if her name is Ryan.

# Gang Associate

They said he was a
"prison gang associate."
He felt proud.
He'd come a long way
from gangsta, banger,
home boy from the 'hood.
He'd shown his wood.

"My associates and I
are gathered here on
this fine evening to
expropriate your funds,
liquidate your assets,
and generally kick your ass."

That's how associates talk,
as everyone knows
in and out of prisons

"Your cooperation
is deeply appreciated –
About six inches deep,
should you wish to know,
In your chest and neck.
if you tell us 'no'."

He takes a bow
then makes a vow:

"So hand over the bling,
let me do my thing;
And you go home to mama,
get to relive the drama."

He'll make partner one day soon
and maybe a corner cell with a view. .

## No Convict Left Behind

We don't leave students behind
No matter how troubled they may be
Why abandon convicts?
Folks once like you and me –
Before slum schools and savage inequity
Set them on a course of angry iniquity
Free of restraint, instruction, direction,
On a one-way street to destruction,
Theirs and ours.

If corrections can't correct,
Correct corrections.
If prisons don't reform,
We've ignored them too long.
Prisons have been around since forever
You'd think we had a lock on this endeavor.

A warehouse is no house of change
Just a junkyard for people and pain;
But prison could be a place of reflection
For the wayward, a route to resurrection.

Instead of the third degree
Give convicts a living degree;
A grade for adjustment, a measure
of our setting, their vetting.
It's all a transaction
focus on the daily action.

Why not Honor the Honorable
With a Certificate of Correction:
A Seal of Good Prison Living
A Stamp of Mature Coping
A Symbol of Growth in Adversity.

Put them on a fast-track to a new life,
Courtesy of a Concerned, Committed, Corrections
Community, Standing by its alumni.

Rehabilitation guaranteed
Defects remedied
Upon return.

Why not Acknowledge the Adequate
With a Certificate of Completion.
They've done their stretch,
Paid their debt,
Set accounts right.
Give them a second bite
At life.

Prospects good
Liberal repair,
Return policy.

Why not Mark the Failures --
the mad
the bad
the terminally inept
all who need to be kept
under the gaze of authority
in prison and out –
With an Incomplete, or better, an
In-Progress Badge, for those
Not yet ready for primetime,
But reachable in due time,
Open to renovation
If we summon the energy,
muster the innovation.

Buyer beware
Emergency recall
Twenty-four, seven.

Progress in Living:
Our most important product.
Some setbacks expected,
Others certifiably corrected.

## Corrections Commencement Ceremony

"Survivor First Class Smith,
reporting for release, sir."
Smith stands erect, chest swelling,
Ready for the coveted C – Corrected,
to be pinned on his crisply pressed shirt.

Call it the Gentleman's C
For those we hope to see
Out and about
Living a good life.

"Survivor Second Class Rodriquez,
reporting for release, sir."
Rodriquez is awarded the enigmatic A – Acceptable,
For those we say
may one day
make their way
Our way.

"Survivor Third Class Jones,
Ready to go."
"Isn't that, 'Ready to go, Sir?' asks the Warden.
"Ready to go, sir," replies Jones.

Awarded the hopeful IP – In Progress,
Jones may one day be
Free, like you and me
To sail in life's rough lee
Stable, free
Amid the tempest of temptation, strife
That was his criminal life.

# Our Tier

Our tier, our town, look around
cells and surround sound;
petulance, flatulence, a tortured tune,
walls ain't coming down any time soon.

But the world comes in
On radio and TV signals
Audible at any decibel
Crashing all around us
Drowning us

In a sea
We can't see
Not clearly
Not really.

# SHU Fly

Lifers lie dormant in prison cells,
some in SHUs,
that's Special Housing Units,
pronounced Shoes,
where prisoners are buried deep
underground,
like cicadas,
stored and ready for resurrection
some 17 years hence
(if they're lucky).

One day they wake up free;
startled, they stumble to life
hands over their eyes
flying blind
carcasses strewn everywhere.

# Florescent Lighting

The prison had standard fluorescent lighting,
little flourished there
under the harsh glare.

The tubes dispelled the darkness
but shed an unflattering light on life,
Revealing scars and lesions,
the occasional suppurating sore.

Even smells seemed worse, somehow,
as if they radiated off dirty, sweaty bodies;
Blinding you with an acrid haze,
Stink that stayed with you for days.

Let there be light!
said the Lord,
Who never did time
in a modern prison.

Let there be florescence!
That would be something.

Fluorescent lights may last for life, but
Florescence, well, that makes life worth living.

# Days of Our Lives
*by Seri Irazola*

"Like sand through the hourglass"
that turned to mud and got stuck
I wait

In a concrete room
with grey walls and floors
and a steel bunk
I wait

On a bed that has held
so many bodies
other than my own
That has tasted semen, blood, tears
other than my own
I wait

For surcease
Release

Relief
from this life
Where sand turned to mud
And time stopped

These are the days of our lives
These are the days of my life.

# VIPs

Virtually Imprisoned Persons
Trapped in images
Drowning in slogans
Bleeding from sound-bites
Worried about their makeup
Not their constitution

Appearances count
Surfaces suffice.

Superficiality
Beats technicality
Image
Beats substance
Pictures
Tame arguments
Belief
One good exposure
Away.

Don't complain or explain
Makes you look lame
Just smile
For the cameras.

Virtually Imprisoned Persons
Trapped in images
Living large
Living tame
Image and substance
One and the same.

## A flickering light

A flickering light in a cell house window
licks the night-stained lime-stone wall,
violating the darkness
like a thief in the night,
stealing peace of mind
from the black hole
convicts call home.

Two men lay within
on cement bunks
framed by bars
cast in shadows
minds in distant places
lost in races they hope one day to run.

They read and dream by a solitary bulb
dangling from above
heads barely hidden beneath thinning hair
free for a time, maybe more free
than they will ever be,

When prison gates close behind them
and they rejoin a world
barred to them
pretty much from the start.

# Years of living alone

Years of living alone
leached the color from her face,
left her as pale as the concrete floor
she paced daily, nightly, ever so lightly
so as not to draw attention to herself,
what was left of her self,
barely visible
behind the  bars
in the afterglow
of lights out
on death row

## Don't let your babies grow up to be convicts

I aim to ride this day down into night
like a bronco that can't be tamed,
to stay up 'til light, to put up a fight
against rules that say
lights out because it's time
wear a saddle, wear this brand,
you're mine, doin' time.

Plenty of time, alright,
but no saddle in sight
no mark on my butt
so I stay up
reading
or just horsing around
looking for enlightenment
looking for a sign
looking for something that's mine,
all mine.

## Old Men

The old men flaunt faded tattoos
that sing of boisterous youths
now fallen fallow on bony arms,
now heaving, rolling, on swollen guts:
Daggers once held firm, at the ready,
hidden, wrapped in shrouds of fat;
Guns, too, holstered in layers of flesh,
hard to reach;
Names of mothers stretched
beyond recognition;
Marriages celebrated, then broken
beyond repair;
Men in decline,
serving time;
Marked by life,
for life.

## Desperately seeking freedom

O'er the cell a mark still lingers
Of where a convict's bloodied fingers
Could make stone speak of life's hard ends
With words that shine like darkling gems
I was here
I am a man
I bleed, therefore I am...
Alive, in a manner of speaking
It's raw, sweet freedom I'm desperately seeking
A prison cell's a coffin reeking
Of dreams gone sour
Of life died by the hour
Of death by decree
Until you're set free
In this life or the next.

## Cell Mate
*by Robert Johnson & Ania Dobrzanska*

I sit before her, crouched
In the corner of our bare cell.
Fully clothed, fully exposed,
Hurt, alone
Head shaking
Heart aching
Thoughts racing.
I am a prisoner –
A prisoner of her rage
A prisoner in her cage
A prisoner of my own private death row
That's how things go
When abuse becomes a way of life
and death.

She looms above me
An animal now with teeth bared
Words that bite, tear my flesh –
I am a whore
I am a slut
I am trash
Unworthy, unwanted.

She grows bigger with each insult
Swelling up, feeding off my pain.
I shrink before her eyes
Dying a little inside.

Later, she snuggles up to me
As if nothing had happened.
"We'll get through this," she purrs.

We?

## On the Yard

Muggers, rapists, robbers and thieves mill about aimlessly, or so it seems, among small-time junkies and dealers with big-time dreams, in occasional conferences, bargaining, overheard but not understood by the nut cases, men in their own orbit, on their own highs, in turn beset by the retarded, who think the crazies are conduits to the gods, think their hallucinations are harbingers of things to come, signs that hold answers to their muttered, stuttered pleas for guidance, direction, relief from the chaos that envelops their days and nights in the prison, a Playstation fantasy world where folks play for keeps and scripts get written and rewritten all the time.

Tattoos form a crazy quilt of sick art, rendered on human flesh, pointing the way to the various and sundry constellations on planet prison, one sadder or madder than the next. This way to gangs and girls (or a reasonable facsimile); that way to muscles with mothers perched on biceps; watch out for guns half hidden by boxer shorts, peeking out at the waist, as if in a holster; beware devils and goblins and serpents, medieval creatures loose on the sagging skin of bearded, ponderous, dangerous men, folk you watch out for, can't befriend.

Follow the yellow brick road but don't show yellow, fellow, or it's a long, long way from Kansas to where you'll be heading, a piece of meat, somebody's bedtime treat.

Primitive. Primeval. Just-plain-evil.

But there it is, there you are, far from home, trying to find a home on the prison range, where life is downright strange, and ain't nobody free.

# Fishing

He baits his hook with
Snacks of all sorts:
Cheese nibs
Chocolate chips
Gums and mints.
And of course
Life Savers,
Sweet Life Savers.
In various flavors
Even Tropical Fruits
Hard to come by in this gray world.

He hopes one of the young ones
Innocent and fair
(Relatively speaking)
Will nibble or bite.
Or at least grab hold of him,
Reach for his outstretched hand,
Grab on for dear life.

For life can be dear,
Even in prison.
And utterly unbearable,
Especially in prison,
When you cast your reel
And the line comes back slack.

Another chance at happiness,
However sad or sordid,
That got away.

## A crown of thorns

A crown of thorns,
shiny, steel, serrated,
rests uneasily atop the walls of his world,
visible through thin windows carved from stone,
narrow slits that offer stunted slices of life
inside and out.

The prison, long and lean, modeled on a telephone pole,
looks like a makeshift crucifix in the dying light of day,
head and feet and hands festooned with towers,
now lit in backdrop, set off against the graying sky,
home to armed guards, guards

Who know not whom they may one day shoot
but know well there is no getting out of this inn
without Caesar's consent.

"Forgive them," he thinks, though these days
forgiveness is not for prisoners to give,
"Even if they know, all too well,
what they do."

# Birthdays in the World

He walks across the dusty ground
hoary with frost so fine
the yard looks like
icing on an old cake;
brittle, broken up,
left over from birthdays
in the world, far from prison.

## Night Fright

He approaches the tawny, tattooed man
with tremulous, tentative steps,
his face a mask of stone.

It is twilight and the moon-soaked ground,
almost luminescent, threatens to give way,
to let him fall right out of this day
out of this place
out of this life.

But the ground stands firm
and he stands firm
feet planted squarely
a shoulder's width apart.

Gently he caresses his shank
(homemade, handmade)
to remind himself where he is
and what he is
and what he must do
to see another day.

# Stone by Stone

The rocky road opens before him,
then wraps around the quarry
from which the prison was built,
stone by stone
man by man
life by life,
each piece of raw material
a wonder of nature,
the end result...
something less.

## Outside it's Christmas

Sheets of ice lock the prison down
like a deadbolt on a cell door,
everyone trapped inside
nowhere to go
the world still
time frozen
men cast in ice
cold as death.

Outside it's Christmas
Inside it's Business.

The New Year Approaches
The Old Year Reproaches.

Prisoners and Keepers,
As One,
Stuck Dumb
By the sheer weight of time.

# Year Book

Head shots arrayed in columns and rows,
monuments to the harsh workings of time:

Characters captured
fates sealed

In tears
on tiers

One life at a time,
lost in time.

## He awakens

He awakens, drinks in the familiar stench,
notes the order of things in his cell –
steel commode, iron bars, cement walls –
feels the muggy warmth of sleeping men,
Then breathes deep the raw wound of emptiness
and retreats into the soul-saving stupor of sleep.
"Wake me when it's over," he thinks,
knowing the day will come too soon.

# World Outside
## *by Chris Miller*

Daily the sparrow lands upon my slatted sill.
Its gentle frame resting nestled in my calloused palm.
It eats scraps scrupulously saved
Gazing quizzically upon my visage
Then its lazy wings unfurl
Guiding in flight towards the limitless horizon

Each day I await the sparrow
He is my proof
Confirmation that life remains upon the globe
Living, breathing, running, flying
Something beyond the monotonous sky
Something beyond the bloodstained walls

I can never fly away
But the sparrow heralds life
To savor, to adore
Transcending captivity
My spirit roams free
I still have a part to play.

Daily the sparrow returns
So long as my eyes can see
So long as I can feed his earthly cravings
Stroke his gentle breast
Life reveals itself
I have something to live for

## Go Straight

Go straight
to your date
with
Poverty
Homelessness
Joblessness
Hopelessness.

Go straight
to jail
Do not pass Go
Do not collect 200 dollars
Do not land on Public Housing.

Go straight
back home
Where lepers roam
scarred, marred
tattooed, screwed
Folk like you.

The Underclass
The Déclassé
Folk we throw away.

# I'll Be Back

"Hasta la vista, baby"
Say we to the departing convict
Ambling out the door
Bus ticket in hand
Dirty clothes on his back,
Sometimes the very same threads he came in with,
stored for years the way they were the day he arrived,
sweaty, bloodstained, a little vomit around the edges.

Flush with money?
No, just flushed.

      10 bucks in viginia,
      50 in maine
      zilch in tennessee

"I'll be back"
says the convict,
smarter than he looks.

# IV.

## DEATH HOUSE

# Good People

"Good people are always so sure they're right,"
said Barbara Graham, one of the last women executed
by the State of California, back in '55,
Immortalized by Susan Hayward in the
classic film, *I Want to Live*. Her last words
may be the last word on capital punishment.
Good people condemning bad people,
Sure they are right, even as
Exonerations mount, even as
We lean heavily, unsteadily
on our hidden execution rite
To get us through one more dark night
And then another...

# The Chair
*by Jennifer Adger*

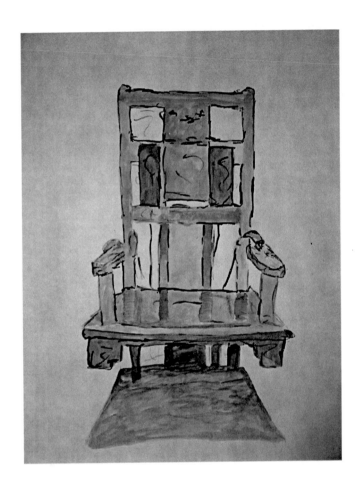

# The Iceman Killeth

The execution-style killer is a pillar
of the prison community.
Cold as ice, hard as steel,
he is admired and feared.
But he pays with his life
counted in empty years on prison tiers,
or a living death on condemned row
before, a broken man, he is taken in tow
to the death house and its chamber of fears.
        Punishment hurts.

The law's executioner is a pillar
of the free community.
Cold as ice, hard as steel,
he is admired and feared.
But he pays with his soul
counted in bad dreams that toll
slowly, during long sleepless nights,
or in mordant cynicism, which like sin
eats at life slowly, from within.
        Punishment hurts.

All of us, made
Cold as ice, hard as steel
unable to feel
the harm we do
in the name of justice.

## Needle Work

Lethal Injection
a deadly intersection
in the search for perfection
in the war on crime.

A dead criminal
silent and still
cradled by catheters,
clinging to a cross.

Lethal Injection
the ultimate rejection
a poison confection
spread over the body of crime.

Condemned criminals
all in a row
suitable for framing.
Unmoving, uncomplaining.

Lethal Injection
a chemical subjection
for people of complexion
whose supine demise
lends authority to lies

Enshrined in law
beyond inspection
beneath reflection
in the search for perfection
in the war on crime.

"They sigh and drift off to sleep," we hear.
"Much worse for their victims," we're told is clear.
"Really nothing to fear," we all exclaim.
How can anyone protest or complain,
in the face justice so tame,
so transparently humane.

Execution day, we pray
brings sweet, sound slumber.
Free of guilt or remorse or regret
we feel sure the number
put to death on prison gurneys
take their final journeys
decently, justly,
as if by personal election
in the search for perfection
in the war on crime.

# Execution Night

My son was born in the morning, days before the execution.
I was there, amid the
blood and the gore, and
the tears of joy.
He cried, I cried, and
the world opened before him.

The condemned man was killed as midnight approached.
I was there, amid the
burned flesh and the yawning, gaping mouth, and
the vacant eyes.
He died, no one cried, and
the world closed around him.

I couldn't help but think of them
together
dearly arrived, dreadfully departed
bookends, brackets
around the day
around existence.

This man before me,
shaved down to his tender skin
an overgrown baby, really

swaddled in denim
strapped to the chair

delivered unto death
in our name.

# Alien Justice

Raise your space helmet visor
if you think Sigourney Weaver is God.
Okay, check your air supply first.

Alexander Williams, a
Georgia death row inmate,
thinks Sigourney Weaver is God.
Does that mean he's crazy?
Officials thought so, and
stayed his execution.

Sigourney Weaver may not be God
nor even a mere Goddess
but she is a force to be reckoned with.

Not a Dark Force
or an Alien Force
or even a Moving Part on an Axis of Evil.

She is, instead, a Wonder Woman
as we have come to know Her
after Women's Liberation
unchained our Sisters
and let them reach for the Stars
and maybe a distant Galaxy or two.

Thanks, Sigourney,
God knows we needed you.
And if you can save just one death row inmate,
so much the better.

Note: Williams subsequently had his sentence commuted. He's been granted life. Ms. Weaver had no comment. None was needed.

# burnt offerings

there
in the damp basement
of the aging prison
near the
chair

death
the scent of
burnt offerings
hangs in the
air

a
devil's brew of
mildew, flesh, and
fear

the
chair is gone
(the latest reform)
the smell lives
on

# A Messy Business

Justice can be a messy business.
We used to torture criminals on the rack
then kill them. To call that justice was a stretch,
but we did, turning levers with abandon.
All righty tighty, no lefty loosey, until the poor wretches
were pulled nearly apart, gaining a few inches
in height, but of course it was excruciating to move
even a little, and impossible to walk. So criminals
weren't taller, they were longer.
Sometimes we'd beat these long-fellows
to the point of death and then
tear them limb from limb
with the help of horses or
men with horse sense and little more.

All this was bloody
and the screams terrible,
even to medieval ears,
but it was great community fun.
We saw the Devil among us
and we had Him on the run.
Villages would fight for the right
to punish, pushing and pulling
and spitting, even biting,
in a preview of tortures to come.
And we think television is violent!

Things are more clinical today,
tame as a housebroken dog.
True, there's still a hanging or two,
an occasional firing squad at dawn,  and
a fair number of electrocutions,
though seating is limited, what with
modern sensibilities holding us back.
Today's executions are bloodless,
victims quiet and still.  No one
on the rack was quiet and still.
And then there were the cheers,
The crowds eager for souvenirs.

Today we doubt the Devil, so
our criminals are small letter types,
as in bad or evil, or even monster,
not Dark Demon or Minion of Satan.
If crime has lost it drama, so has punishment.
We rely on lethal injection in most cases.
No one knows what it's like, of course,
but no one ever does with execution.
Or cares. All these changes in methods
were for me and you, the viewing public.
We used to like blood and gore,
and screaming in stereo, so
stones and clubs, swords and fire
worked just fine. Now we want
a tame death scene,
a tableau of criminals
looking alive but dead
like people well waked.
"He never looked better," we might say
of the average dead man walking.
Maybe people do say that.
I'm sure they think it. Especially
when they think of the victim, who,
in timeless fashion, dies screaming
amid blood, sweat and tears,
awash in pools of feces and urine and vomit.

The image of condemned criminals
in peaceful, waxy repose is the
real appeal of lethal injection.
A pinprick, maybe a gasp for air,
but never a mark on them.
No surface blemishes; no signs of pain.
We want death domesticated, emasculated,
so lethal injection is the ticket.

But what next? Whither the technology
of state-made death?
We could use lasers, but someone would
have to point the beam. Looks wild, aggressive,
implicates us in an act of violence. God forbid
we should kill people and feel
implicated in an act of violence.

One candidate: the ubiquitous microwave.
We hesitate, understandably, feeling squeamish.
There is the nasty association with ovens,
which brings to mind the Nazis
and their primitive ovens, but we did
use gas for a spell, and we put offenders
in capsules not all that different from ovens,
so we can get over this.
You don't see human rights activists
shunning the microwave, do you?
They zap their food as often as regular folk, maybe more,
since they have to be out all day protesting injustice
while the rest of us can go home and watch TV,
letting our food simmer over a real flame,
stirring during commercials.

The beauty of execution by microwave is that
it's a clean, quiet killer – it cooks the life out of you
without doing any visible damage to the body,
at least that the naked eye can see, and remember,
it's only the visible body that matters. What you see
is what you get. An added bonus, justice consumers:
we can cook the condemned  and eat our dinner, too,
without so much as the touch of a human hand
on the newly departed.

So I propose a small, crisp salute – a micro-wave –
to a new frontier in capital punishment.
True, we're treating felons like animals,
but they're dead meat anyway, aren't they?

## Dead Letter Law

Habeas Corpus, the Great Writ,
the Get-Out-of-Jail-Free bit,
If they bite, spitting up the body,
slightly chewed but undigested,
more or less whole.

But the Great Writ, now
thanks to Congress, really
a late writ, a writ-small
writ, hardly a writ-at-all writ.

Habeas is a corpse, man,
so much dead letter law,
at least in capital cases.
You get the body back
in a box or a bag,
death the only release.

Un-appealing, but that's how
Capital appeals go these days.
'Cause we're terror crazy
and too scared or lazy
or maybe just too hasty
to see the nasty chalk outline
drawn around the law.

## Postcard from Death Row

Single room, grate view
round-the-clock room service
uniformed security staff
all utilities, medical and dental covered.

Last meal special –
open menu, all you can eat.

Wish you were here!

# Small Talk

"Did you ever hold a knife and know it was just right?" he asked, sitting across from me in the room adjoining the death chamber. "It's the handle, the shape of the handle. And the thickness. Yeah. And the edge. Like this one beauty had a top blade, you know, with teeth facing backward..."

"A hunter's knife," I added, without thinking, not sure I wanted to be a part of this conversation.

"Yeah. That's it. This one time, the knife was perfect, man. It went in deep and smooth, cut clean, real clean. Then came out rough, ragged."

He smiled, then said, with boyish enthusiasm. "You know that had to hurt!"

I figured as much, but said nothing. When I didn't reply, he said, "Did you ever hold a gun and just know..."

# The Big Hurt

Death by automation
Pain by remote control.
Distant, impersonal,
Machine-tooled, Factory-fresh,
Mechanized Executions.

Reliable
Guaranteed
Check warranty for details.

Here's how it works:
A conveyor belt
run to death row
ferries flaccid felons
carb-fed, half-dead,
plucked, shucked,
routed on ramps
everybody amped.

Featuring our Patented,
No-Touch System:
Loading Robots (L-Bots)
Place Package (Offender) on belt,
Receiving Robots (R-Bots)
accept, then transfer Package to
Terminal Robots (T-Bots),
ever-ready, ever-revved,
Programmed in mega-hertz
to deliver the Big Hurt
On demand.

Assembly-line slaughter
something to see
Robots L, R & T --
better than TV.

Some assembly required
Powers down automatically
Stores well.

## Last supper

A fried steak, diced into little squares,
arrives at the death house,
neatly reassembled, like a puzzle,
laid to rest in the center berth
of a standard white styrofoam box,
bordered on one side by soggy, sagging fries,
on the other by wilted greens, curled and brown,
long past their salad days, like the man himself,
who ordered this meal as the sad celebration,
culmination, of a dreary, wasted life
that it is even now slipping away,
as he ages before our eyes right there in his cell,
called "the last night cell" in some prisons,
"the death cell" in this one.

Later, he will be cooked, in a manner of speaking,
in the electric chair, but not diced or reassembled,
before he is boxed without frills in a plywood coffin,
the mortuary's answer to the styrofoam box, and
buried in the prison cemetery, home to the
most common and indigestible waste
of the prison system.

He eats alone with a plastic fork –
no knives for the condemned,
no dinner companions for the condemned –
chewing carefully, kneeling by his bed, as if in
genuflection before the raw power of the state,
his meager meal placed carefully on the steel gray metal bed,
sitting precariously on the top sheet, drawn tight
like a sail battened down for heavy weather.

We look at each other tentatively, almost furtively,
lawyers, chaplains, even officers speaking in low tones,
words directed toward the ground,
as if we are greasy, dirty, our mouths dry,
tongues swollen, sticking to our teeth,

our noses stinging from the scent of corruption,
the bittersweet stink of fear in the air,
in our hair, on our skin, in our clothes.

We are guests at a living wake,
where the dead live,
where the dead see,
look you in the eye and see nothing,
see no one will save them
see they are utterly alone.

The condemned man finishes his meal,
says 'thank you' to the officers who fed him dinner,
and later walks with them to his execution, on schedule,
dead before the stroke of midnight. We go home,
stomachs empty, hungry for sleep.

## Like the French

Maryland executes people like the French did,
Not with a guillotine but during a given week,
With no warning of the day or time.

"The condemned shall be executed During the Week of X,"
Maryland Officials solemnly proclaim, Where X
Marks the end of your sorry life and
We're sorry we can't give you the particulars;
have to worry about security, crowds, publicity –
So we keep the press guessing
And your loved ones
And of course you.

We don't serve special last meals, either.
We don't want to be confused with the French
Who probably fed the condemned something delightful,
Cutting edge cuisine on the eve of the guillotine.
A last meal to be remembered, if not by prisoner,
Then by a society that savors each meal
As if it were the last morsel of pleasure
Served up in this life.

No, in the Maryland death house we serve what's on the regular
prison menu, which is on par with dog food.
Almost, anyway.
Dog food comes in many varieties,
Dry and wet, some for tender tummies.
A few have yoghurt mixed in.
Prison food is pretty much one size fits all. Badly.
Stuff is so worked over you'd think it was digested and
Served up from an intestine near you.

Don't coddle the condemned
Don't eat with them either.

The day you get a really, really
Bad meal on death row is probably your last –
Last taste of Maryland
A sorry imitation of France
Where we hold the Freedom Fries

And other Free World treats
On some principle I can't follow, and
Decent folk find hard to swallow.

## Last night lullaby

Good night moon
Good night gloom
Good night uniform and plastic spoon
Good night keeper of this chilly tomb

Good night cell
Good night smell
Good night screams of man and bell
Good night tiers in this living hell

Good night tears that each night fell
Quietly, privately, on my pillow
Hidden from the other fellow
Struggling, too, with dreams gone fallow

Good night moon
Good night gloom
Good night to my metal cocoon
(too cold for me to call a womb)
Tomorrow brings release from pain
A new life ready to bloom again.

## when the gurney comes for you

death row ain't that bad, he said,
but what did he know
he was homeless at 9.

needle ain't that bad, he said,
but what did he know
he was a junkie at 12.

i got hope, he said, life ain't that bad
but what did he know
his life ended long ago
long before death row,

starting with a child-mother who bore him
with labor pains and growing pains
and a life bound to whim, not him.

at the end he said, death ain't that bad,
i'll be strong, get thru,
this much he thought he knew
a certain wisdom born, he said,
when the gurney comes for you.

# Hope?

"You gave me hope," he said, looking hopeful, almost cheerful. "I'd given up, you know, thrown in the towel, said 'this is it.' And it was. You could say I was ready. I'd accepted it, not that it was easy. But I saw it coming and I was ready to throw myself under the bus. Or stand right out in front of it. And I was numb, just didn't care. Then you gave me hope. Now, right now, I have hope."

I nodded, feeling a little queasy.

"You guys care. I feel like I'm alive. The past, well, it just don't hurt as much. I can forgive, even if I can't forget. Forgive her. My mom. She was just a child when she had me, and when she left me in the streets. Homeless. Forgive myself, for what I turned out to be. A junkie, mugger, murderer of helpless old women. Well, only one woman but she was a grandmother and her grandchildren were in the car. The car I tried to steal before all hell broke loose and she was dead and I was dead, or at least sentenced to death. But I'm not done yet. I can still be somebody. I can redeem myself. I have hope."

Sitting on death row, smiling at a man I'd come to know and like, I shared that hope, even reveled in it. At first. Fighting the death penalty; it's the good fight, right? Hopeful. I was hopeful. Uneasy, even at the outset, because this is a big deal, but hopeful. And that hope stayed with me long after that visit. Even as his appeals were denied and his bids for commutation were denied and even his requests for extended last visits were denied, I clung to the hope that he had hope and that there were grounds for hope, even if I couldn't see them anymore. On the last day, as the hours ticked down, I had hope that he had hope and that there were grounds for hope, even if couldn't see them anymore.

I see him sometimes, if I let my mind wander, standing in his cell, ten feet from the execution chamber, hopeful – hopeful for a last minute visit, maybe even a last-minute reprieve. If I try hard, I see him on the gurney, and with a herculean effort, I cling to the hope that he had hope and there were grounds for hope, right up until the end. Even though it was hopeless, maybe from the start.

The end came and he went to his death and he went alone, so it's hard to cling to the hope that he had hope even when there were no grounds for hope, even when the lethal chemicals made their way into his body. And even now, I hope he forgave me for being one of the bearers of false hope who left him very much alone at the end. That's the last hope in this hopeless undertaking, and I cling to this hope, even if there are no grounds for hope when you get real close to the death house.

# Little Miracles
*by Sonia Tabriz*

So as I sit here I wonder,
is this really all there is?

Little obsessions.

Empty thrills we create for ourselves
and magnify in our minds
to distract us from despair;
from the fear we feel
that these creations all around us,
that surround us,
are nothing.

Because in the end
each of us will live and die alone.

Nothing conveys.

We live.

We die.

And the details,
what happens in the middle,
doesn't really bear weight.

At the end of the day
your day
my day
these little distractions are all we have.

Minor miracles to live by
in your house
my house
even the death house.

# V.

## CARNAGE
## AND
## CONSEQUENCES

## Global Village Life

The image of the world as
one big Global Village
has appeal to us, folks
who've mostly never lived in a village.

Getting to know something
about everyone on the planet
sounds so connected, so authentic.
Who could resist?

We forgot about village idiots
and about chronic malcontents
whose stupidity and bad temper
can wreak havoc on our lives.

Worse, we forgot about victims
of injustice, real and imagined,
whose resentments simmer and boil
just below the surface of village life.

And worst of all, we forgot that our Global Village
was a stepchild of technology,
not the flowering of community.

A place where guns and bombs
and hijacked planes
can be weapons of terror
wielded by the wounded,
who make it their life's work to
annihilate  innocents at will
in numbers beyond comprehension.

Misery has always loved company.
It used to be that the miserable
had only each other's company.
Now, in our cozy Global Village,
the forlorn and the rejected,
the isolate and the fanatic,
see the happy, chosen peoples
at close range,

Even if only on TV, radio, or Internet,
like targets in a shooting gallery
or in a video game of doom.
Some of them take aim,
and the rest is history.

# Living Planet
*by Eleanor Potter*

## It takes a child...

Operation Infinite Justice
has long now winged its worrisome way
East, crossing continents and cultures,
menacing peoples alien to us
and us to them.

Finite bombs have fallen,
and may yet fall, inflicting
infinite suffering
in retribution for our
infinite suffering.
Innocents perish
in punishment
for the perishing
of innocents.

War, we are told,
is the way of history,
the way to Enduring Peace.
But we could rewrite history
as we enter the 21th century,
waging not war, but peace –
a campaign against global injustice, the
dark mother of desperate deeds

Peace means inclusion, then connection.
Inclusion makes growing fields
instead of killing fields.
Connection shores up islands of possibility
in an ocean of goodwill.
Children know these things,
learned hard but learned well
in every kindergarten and playground
on the planet.

If it takes a village to raise a decent child,
it may take a child's sense of decency
to make our world – the Global Village –
a decent place to live.

# Dial nine-one-one, Believe

Nine-one-one
planes crashing into
buildings collapsing onto
people on the run.

Nine-eleven
drop to your knees,
pray to heaven.

Nine-one-one
smoke and rubble covering
molten graves fusing
flesh and steel as one.

Nine-eleven
drop to your knees
pray to heaven.

Nine-one-one
mass murder makes
mass media makes
masses numb.

So many killed
so many times.

So many bereft.
Is there anyone left
untouched?

Nine-one-one
a day to remember, of
a bygone September, when
we came together as one
People.

Nine-eleven
drop to your knees,
pray to heaven.

## A ZOO NEAR YOU

Thank God
if you can still
believe.

# Modern Mariners, We?

Enemies, enemies, everywhere
Nary a moment to think.

Enemies, enemies, everywhere
Oh, how the world does shrink.

Enemies, enemies, everywhere
Watch what you open, eat or drink.

Enemies, enemies, everywhere
Are we on the brink?

What Albatross did we selfishly shed
to have so many wanting us dead?

Is it our madness for modernity?
Our material immaturity?

Or our secrets, like Victoria's,
so publicly displayed?

That make us reprehensible, indefensible,
a source of endless enmity and envy
to much of the world?

Enemies, enemies, everywhere
our best hope is to persevere,
affirming values we hold dear,

Freedom in its varied forms,
some tasteful, others tasteless,
all utterly delicious.

## The Terrorist in the Guest Room

Terrorists flying planes
into landmark buildings
slaughtering thousands in their wake
is nothing if not surreal,
the stuff of nightmares
one wakes up from in
a cold sweat.

The Taliban, a surreal group by any Western measure,
played their part, claiming they couldn't release Osama,
the likely mastermind of this madness,
and a war even now still with us because...
he was their guest.

Their guest! Of course! Had we forgotten our manners?
Don't we all have the occasional terrorist over for a spell?
When pressed, don't we, like good hosts the world over,
find a place in our homes for the occasional mass murderer
       for the fanatic in the family room
       or the bomber in the basement
who come calling of a fine September day?

To the Taliban and Al Qaeda and others like them,
America is The Great Satan,
The Malevolent Mecca of Modernity,
Home to The Evil Trinity:

Towers of American Greed, not mutual World Trade
Manse of Military Might, not Shield of Fragile Freedom
House of Dark License, not Guardian of Liberty and Light

They couldn't understand us less
or misunderstand us more
if they tried.

# Stretched on Iraq

pulled apart
torn asunder

war wary
war weary

walking wounded
dead to carry

human remains
shimmering in the sun

each grain,
each glint, once

a grand
husband, wife,
son, daughter

to dust
now returned
in short order.

peace offerings
piece offerings
surcease
release.

## Desert Grave

Abu Ghraib
Iraqi dungeon
American grave?

For whom?
Open the tomb
Turn the lens to zoom
Let's all have a look, see.

Could it be...
Rumsfeld, rumbling?
Powell, posturing?
Rice, reproving?
Bush, butchering...?
        The Geneva Convention.

Or just some lowly grunts
Fixed in the cross hair
Caught in the harsh glare
Judged too dirty
Now the dirty work is
Done

# Dueling Deities

Dueling Deities
demanding discrimination.
Precious Pieties
polluting proprieties.

God on the end
of every sword and pen,
declaiming the end
of life as we know it,
for the sinner in the other
station, nation, congregation.

Damnation
It's all the rage these days.

If zealots weren't as common as fleas
Humankind might find its ease
in one another, without theology
hiding our shared  genealogy
which makes you and me, us and him
a Siamese twin, under the skin.

# Jihadi Gras

Osama bin Laden came
laden with treats
Christian Kabobs, Hebrew meats,
Fettuccini Al Queda
A killer feast.

Hamas brought the hummus
No chick peas, please
Chicks and parties
Don't mix, they believe.

Hizbollah brought baklava
Covered in balaclavas
Straight from Ramallah.
What great fellahs!

A merry time was had by all
'Til Sami the suicide bomber,
head wrapped too tight,
burst onto the scene.

"This party was the bomb,"
he'd been told, "a demented
Global Village Prom."
So he razed the roof,
looking for virgins
and ultimate truth.

In the aftermath
in the cold light of day, as
dreams of deliverance fade away –
like smoke from burning rubble
like blood from streets awash in tears
each of us drowning in our mortal fears,

We might one day say, Terrible,
But true, what we do,
when we close our eyes
when we live by lies
dead certain we're right

that only our light
our religious rendition
dispels the dark night
soothes the human condition.

## V-Days

V is for Victory
Hopes George, a
Burning Bush
Yearning to
Vanquish Evil, maybe
Vindicate Dad.

V is for Villain,
Senses Saddam, a
Sad man, a Mad man,
A Force for Venality
in his Arid Principality.

V is for Victim
Knows the Iraqi man on the street.
Violation a way of life –
first homegrown guns and germs and strife,
now foreign planes and heaps of rubble,
an endless vista of pain and trouble.

V is for Valium
given to children
like candy, by
helpless parents, hoping
drugged dreams will

Cushion the Shock,
Mute the Awe, of
America's Modern war, where

Military monsters, red
in tooth and claw,
like dragons spew forth fire
hot and raw,
and with licking tongues
beckon, threaten, blacken
every door

By dark of desert days,
amid the wind- and

bomb-fed haze;
by bright of desert nights,
lit by missiles in flight.

A Martial Spectacular, in
Living Color and Surround Sound,
Playing in the Theater of War
They call home.

# Postscript

As the War Cools Down
(and Ethnic Tensions Heat Up)
V is for Vacuum,
of Power and Order,
maybe Hope.

Iraq, now a Hollow Place,
Void at its Core, like the
Empty Space
Inside the
Statue of Saddam,
Pulled to the Ground,
Dragging Down
This Vacant Man, who
Brought a Kingdom
To its Knees, and
Cast a Civilization into
a Desert of Despair.

# Living Free is the Best Revenge

We're asked to give up civil rights
in the fight against terrorism.
People are dying for us,
can't we make sacrifices, too?

And aren't we just facing reality?
Civil rights suit civil times;
martial rights, martial times.
Aliens and Traitors, mostly people of hue,
deserve only the justice we're wont to do.

But in a free society, aren't
civil rights and human rights
one and the same,
in good times and in bad,
in war and in peace,
'til death do us part?

We may stop being civil
when we're at war, but
we never stop being human.

If some of us must die for freedom,
the rest of us should live it,
every day, in every way,
we can.

## A Nation of Laws?

John Adams famously said,
America is a nation of laws, not men.
Trouble is, we have more laws than men;
more laws than men, women, and children;
more laws, maybe, than sense.

Suspected terrorists have broken the law, we're told,
that's why hundreds are held incommunicado.
But one can hardly walk down the street
without breaking some law.

Any stroll on any block
can become a line-up,
what cops call a "perp walk."

That's not terrorism, I'll grant you,
but it is scary.

## Assume the Position

Hands up,
eyes down,
faces blank.

Bending to the law,
Spreading the message :

"Search Me"
We all say
One way or another.

Submission,
Not petition, the
main position

on the matter
of justice that really
matters

when we look
the other
way.

# Felon du Jour

"Authorities grilled Malvo for seven hours,"
read the headline about the loquacious young sniper suspect.
Meanwhile, a mute Muhammad, moody mastermind, apparent
parent, marinated in his own juices,
sautéing in his solitary cell.

Fresh fish and seasoned mentor will be filleted
in due course and served to a hungry public
when the time is ripe.

Note: Lee Boyd Malvo and John Muhammad were convicted of several
murders following sniper attacks they conducted in the Washington, DC
area in the fall of 2002.

# One Shot Away

Left for Dead
Right for Life
Dead on Arrival
Consumed by Strife
Story of a Life.

Sordid, trite, but
for the gun, the
big, long gun.

The great equalizer
The great tranquilizer
of the human conscience.

DOA
5 one day, at least
six more to pay
snipers at play

Yet two got away
reason to pray

Rest of us anxious
ducking and jiving
struggling and conniving
getting on with each day,
knowing our maker's
but one shot away.

# Terminator

He's a maverick moral cop
is our James Kopp.
In thrall to Jesus,
above it all, he takes the law
into his own hands,
hands holding  high a
high powered rifle, aiming
high, chest and head
high, high on grace,
high on something,
hiding in plain sight
in Caesar's court,
lost in a baggy suit, a
moronic smirk on an
oddly tilted head,
cocked to one side
big glasses resting uneasily
on a narrow face, windows
to a narrow mind.

He stands straight when he shoots,
head oddly tilted,
cocked to one side,
but no smile, not yet.
He's busy stalking his game
tracking them in God's name,
right to the nest, killing them
in front of their chicks, claiming to be
the best sort of Christian:
Protector of the Unborn
Terminator of Terminators
Killer for a Cause
Willing to murder
Without pause
Or compunction
Or compassion.

Abortion, Murder,
Moral contortion

Emotional Fervor
Choreographed Carnage
Close to home.

Note:    James Kopp confessed to murdering Barnard Slepian, an obstetrician who performed abortions as part of his medical practice

## September Storm

Beds of burning charcoal –
pulsating, throbbing,
loiter on the horizon
up to no good.

Full-on storm clouds –
churning, roiling,
lurk overhead, low
over the water.
Thick, tufted,
puffed out,
so many dark predators
heavy with menace.

Threads of mist,
fine as spun sugar,
laced across the sky
like lassos in flight,
frame the scene.

Nature's silver lining.
"This, too,
shall pass."

# VI.

## CLOSING THOUGHTS

# empty spaces
*by Sonia Tabriz*

in this state
between sleep and wake
I ponder the pains of others
in places so far from my own
lingering
in the very same mental space
the break

between daily distraction and sweet escape
from a pain that awaits
and a fear to face

loneliness
too real for us to take
that perhaps
this is it

Recipient of Tacenda Literary Award, Best Poem, 2008

## Thin Blue Line
*by Robert Johnson & Sonia Tabriz*

Cops and ozone
hold the phone
we need a universal 911
to keep the world in line.

Or at least in focus
so we see what ails us,
what tails us –
down the street, in the clouds
overhead, underground

in our hearts
in our heads
a fear of the empty spaces we dread.

Do not cross the line –
the thin blue line,
between us and cosmic chaos,
us and earthly crime

the delicate divide
between us and dead time.

# Beaten in Eden

Adam and Eve sinned pretty much
right out of the chute
but disobedience, deception,
misappropriation of fruit?

Deviance of a menial sort
essentially a contract tort
even with God right there
in the tall reeds.

But no forgiveness, no reconciliation,
the human condition poised for perdition
here and here-after.

Monarchs, would-be Gods in earlier times,
drew up laundry lists of capital crimes,
hanging their dirty linen in the public square,
blood-soaked, tear-stained, a hellish affair.

Our Puritan forebears, upright, uptight,
looked for Satan, found him each night
making auditions and confirming suspicions
in the Wild Woods of the New World.

Their Salem Witch Hunt –
mock trials, mock sins,
pure Mischief even then,
Set the Gold Standard for revenge,
one we've revisited time and again,
most recently with Demon Rum and
Drugs in the Slum, and pretty nearly every
Raisin in the Sun.

Here's a simple history lesson:
we can do better than repression,
which bars people  from the light of day
excludes them from our way.

Prison makes the metaphor real,
a matter of concrete and steel.

187

Reification and, over time,
a prison nation.

Poetic justice, then,
amounts to this:
Sanctions that harden
started in the Garden
We were Beaten in Eden,
rooted out like weeds;
hence the seeds
of discontent
spread so widely;
hence the flowers
of forgiveness
spread so thin.

Which raises a question
in the inquiring mind,
Is it the punishment
or is it the crime
fueling the resentments
of our time?

Is it crime and punishment
that go hand in hand?
Or does punishment feed the crime
that plagues our land?

Reconciliation or revenge?
On this choice
Our future may hinge.

# ABOUT THE AUTHOR & CONTRIBUTORS

**Robert Johnson** (Author) is a Professor of Justice, Law and Society at American University and Editor of BleakHouse Publishing. Johnson is a widely published author of fiction and non-fiction. He is the author of three collections of original poems: *Poetic Justice: Reflections on the Big House, the Death House, and the American Way of Justice*, winner of the L.I.F.E. award from WilloTrees Press; *Burnt Offerings: Poems on Crime and Punishment*; and *Sunset Sonata: Stories and Poems from the River's Edge*. His book, *Lethal Rejection: Stories on Crime and Punishment* (co-edited with Sonia Tabriz), features many of his short stories and plays. Johnson's creative writing has appeared in *Admit2, The American Review, Black Bear Review, The National Catholic Reporter, Carnelian, CMC* (Crime Media Culture), *Dan River Anthology, JMWW, Lifelines, Mannequin Envy, Pleasant Living Magazine, Tacenda Literary Magazine,* and *Wild Violet*. His short story, "The Practice of Killing," won a national fiction contest sponsored by *Wild Violet* magazine. His first novel, *Miller's Revenge*, is in production with Brown Paper Publishing. Johnson's best known work of social science—*Death Work: A Study of the Modern Execution Process*—won the Outstanding Book Award of the Academy of Criminal Justice Sciences.

**Jennifer Adger** (Contributor) is an award-winning artist whose work can be found in private collections in Alabama, California, the District of Columbia, Massachusetts, New York, and Virginia. Some of her work can be seen at www.jenniferadger.net. Adger received her Bachelor's Degree in Psychology from Auburn University and a Masters in Public Policy, with a concentration in Criminal Justice Policy, from the Kennedy School of Government at Harvard University. She is a doctoral candidate in Justice, Law and Society at American University.

**Liz Calka** (Contributor) is an undergraduate student at American University majoring in Visual Media and minoring in Graphic Design. She also is a poet and an award-winning photographer whose works have been featured in *Admit2* and *American Literary Magazine*. Calka designed the cover for Erin George's, *A Woman Doing Life*, as well as the cover for Robert Johnson's, *Miller' Revenge*. She is the architect of the BleakHouse

Publishing website, where her photographs can be found in the online art gallery.

**Ania Dobrzanska** (Contributor) holds a B.A. in Psychology and Administration of Justice from Rutgers University and an M.S. in Justice, Law & Society from American University. She is a Certified Corrections Manager, a designation conferred by the American Correctional Association. Dobrzanska has published several articles in *Corrections Today* on issues of professionalism in corrections and leadership. She is co-author of a chapter on the history of prisons in *Prisons: Today and Tomorrow*, a widely used text; and co-author of an article on the adjustment of life-sentence prisoners published in *Corrections Compendium*, a peer-reviewed journal. Dobrzanska is also a published writer of fiction. Her short story, "Dances with Dragons: Memories of the Hole," appears in *The Crying Wall*, a book she co-edited, and is reprinted in *Lethal Rejection: Stories on Crime and Punishment*.

**Seri Irazola** (Contributor) is a Research Associate I with the Urban Institute's Justice Policy Center. Dr. Irazola has more than five years of research experience in the fields of criminology and social policy. Her interests focus on inmate re-entry, recidivism, impact and conditions of incarceration, crime communities, violence, and victimization. Prior to joining the Justice Policy Center's team at the Urban Institute, Dr. Irazola was a Statistician for the Bureau of Justice Statistics, a branch of the U.S. Department of Justice, Office of Justice Programs. She received her Doctorate and Masters from American University in Washington, DC, and her Bachelors from the University of Michigan.

**Chris Miller** (Contributor) is an award-winning writer specializing in poetry and nonfiction prose. He maintains a strong interest in prison reform and often uses writing as a means to advocate for those whose voices remain unheard. Miller is currently a junior at American University's School of Public Affairs, double majoring in Political Science and Law in Society. He hopes to become a criminal defense attorney.

**Eleanor Potter** (Contributor) is a teacher currently living in Cardiff, Wales. She has a BA Honours degree in Fine Art from the University of Wales in Aberystwyth. She grew up in the

Washington D.C. area and after graduating with the International Baccalaureate from the Washington International School, Eleanor completed her art foundation course at the Wimbledon School of Art in London, U.K. She has had her work displayed at the Goethe Institute in Washington D.C. as well as at exhibitions in the London area.

**Sonia Tabriz** (Contributor) is an honors student at American University majoring in Law & Society and Psychology, the Managing Editor of BleakHouse Publishing, and the Editor-In-Chief of *Tacenda Literary Magazine*. Tabriz was twice awarded the American University Outstanding Honors Student Award and was awarded the American University Multicultural Affairs & International Student and Scholar Services 'Academic Award' for her exemplary scholastic achievements and community involvement. Tabriz recently received the BleakHouse Publishing Fellowship. Her short story titled "The Prison Librarian" (with Victor Hassine) and her poem "empty spaces" have received Tacenda Literary Awards for Best Collaboration and Best Poem, respectively. Tabriz's book, *Lethal Rejection: Stories on Crime and Punishment* (co-edited with Robert Johnson), showcases many of her original writings. Her fiction has also appeared in a number of literary journals including *BleakHouse Review*, *Tacenda Literary Magazine*, and *Admit2*. Tabriz's color drawing, "Hope Behind Bars," served as the cover art for the Spring 2009 edition of *Tacenda Literary Magazine* and her painting, "Hate Behind Bars," served as the cover art for *Miller's Revenge*. She has also designed the text for several books and publications. Tabriz is best known for her fiction and art but has also published works of general and legal commentary.

# OTHER BOOKS BY ROBERT JOHNSON

## Social Science

Culture and Crisis in Confinement

Condemned to Die

Hard Time

Death Work

The Pains of Imprisonment

Crime and Punishment

A Life for a Life

Life without Parole

A Woman Doing Life

## Fiction

The Crying Wall

Justice Follies

Lethal Rejection

Miller's Revenge

## Poetry

Poetic Justice

Burnt Offerings

Sunset Sonata

# PRAISE FOR *POETIC JUSTICE* (2004)

"Prison life is dirty, deadly, treacherous and invisible to all but its inhabitants. Abstractions from outsiders, even well-meaning outsiders, never reveal a prison's shadow side. But Robert Johnson's poetry is different. Chameleon-like, Johnson assumes the spirit and voice of prison survivors to provide an authentic and compelling expression of the day-to-day reality of prison life."

> *Victor Hassine*, a life sentence prisoner now deceased, was the author of *Life without Parole: Living in Prison Today*, as well as many works of fiction.

"Drawing upon years of study and research about crime, punishment, imprisonment and the death penalty, criminologist and social scientist Robert Johnson has produced a powerful, vivid and beautiful collection of poems. Johnson's poetry is as provocative and subtle as his prose."

> *Rita J. Simon*, University Professor, School of Public Affairs, American University, is a noted social scientist who has written over fifty books on law and society.

# PRAISE FOR *BURNT OFFERINGS* (2007)

"Robert Johnson [takes] his readers on an elegiac journey from crime to arrest to confession to trial and ultimately to prison. The book is startling for both its poetic fluency and its stark accuracy... "

> *Charles Huckelbury* is a life sentence prisoner and author of *Tales from the Purple Penguin*, among many other works of fiction and social commentary.

"Johnson expresses the life borne by many entombed within the system. They cannot speak for themselves. Their experiences have silenced them. But like a surgeon, Johnson deftly exposes the sepsis that is the penal system of our ostensibly progressive society... Each poem compels its readers to hear Johnson's voice, as well as the voices of those who too often remain unheard... "

> *Erin George* is a life sentence prisoner and an award-winning poet. She is the author of Origami Heart, a collection of her poems, ,as well as A Woman Doing Life, a work of ethnography about prison life.

"Robert Johnson has opened a window onto an alien, forbidding landscape that is as far from the world the rest of us inhabit as Poe's "El Dorado." We are brought into the world of concertina wire and steel, the world of broken men and women longing for human touch and kindness with such power that we are forced to see and feel what Americans have chosen to ignore far too long: we are warehousing humans behind those walls... [Written] with style and power... *Burnt Offerings* will not be forgotten."

> *Susan Nagelsen* is a Professor of Writing at New England College as well as a widely published author. Her most recent book is *Exiled Voices: Portals of Discovery*.

# BleakHouse Publishing

NEC Box 67
New England College
Henniker, New Hampshire 03242
*www.BleakHousePublishing.com*

**Editor**
Robert Johnson

**Managing Editor**
Sonia Tabriz

**Artistic Director**
Liz Calka

**Senior Consulting Editor**
Susan Nagelsen

**Consulting Editors**
Rachel Cupelo
Christopher Dum
Erin George
Charles Huckelbury
Shirin Karimi
Chris Miller
Jonas Varnum

**Publisher**
Melissa Lang

LaVergne, TN USA
09 December 2010
207978LV00010B/18/P